Valerie Azinge

Founder of My Digital Kitchen

30-Minute
Low-Carb
Dinners

75 *Easy-to-Prepare Meals*
that are Healthy, Delicious and Fast

PAGE STREET
PUBLISHING CO.

PAGE STREET
PUBLISHING CO.

First published in 2020 by
Page Street Publishing Co.
27 Congress Street, Suite 105
Salem, MA 01970
www.pagestreetpublishing.com

Distributed by Macmillan, sales in Canada by The Canadian Manda Group.

24   23   22   21   20   1   2   3   4   5

ISBN-13: 978-1-62414-954-2
ISBN-10: 1-62414-954-5

Library of Congress Control Number: 2019943008

Cover and book design by Ashley Tenn for Page Street Publishing Co.
Photography by Valerie Azinge, Yasaman Shafiei and Kabir Ali

Printed and bound in China

For you, who picked up this book and turned to the first page.

All of your support, interest, encouragement or curiosity,
I am grateful for all of it.

Table of Contents

Introduction

Throughout the years, I've managed to maintain an easy and healthy relationship with food. Whenever I go grocery shopping or heat up the skillet on the stovetop, I always recite this simple equation I made up: "healthy food + boring = myth." This is my mantra for all foods that are wholesome, colorful and delicious. Isn't it awesome? I mean I know it's definitely not math-genius certified, but that's not the goal here.

The challenging part of following a low-carb diet is having to operate at a calorie deficit, which can be even more challenging because of the tendency to get hungrier or fatigued. As I developed recipes for this cookbook, I focused on the necessary nutritional components in each meal to create a healthy balance of macronutrients. These delicious and nutritious recipes will keep you fuller for longer and give your body the energy it requires, especially when it is in its rest state.

I've been a healthy foodie for a while, which is the concept behind my food blog—My Digital Kitchen. But I got into a motorcycle accident that caused a shift in my life. The accident caused some weight gain, muscle loss and some physical limitations that prevented me from exercising like I used to. I knew I needed to establish a new and revamped eating pattern. The solution was to create healthy recipes that were low carb, practical and quick.

I started cutting down my carb intake and limited my diet to high proteins, good fats and low complex carbs. The process wasn't as smooth sailing as before, when my diet was combined with physical activity, but it was still possible to shed the weight, detox my body and reset my metabolism just by eating the right kind of food. When you think about it, it really all begins and ends with food. And no matter what curveballs life throws at me, my relationship with food has always been a happy and healthy one.

With *30-Minute Low-Carb Dinners,* I will introduce you to a selection of beautiful dishes that are healthy and oh so delicious. And you can have them ready in 30 minutes or less. Whether you are trying to lose weight, get healthier, want a fuss-free lifestyle, are a busy professional looking for quick weeknight dinners or you simply love to cook or entertain, this cookbook will be right up your alley and will guide you on all your cooking adventures. Plus, some of the toughest critics I know and love have taste tested these recipes—and they wouldn't have made it into the cookbook if they weren't delicious.

So, it is my humble hope that these dishes inspire you to form a happy and healthy relationship with food, just the same way they helped me through the years. Pull up a chair and join me, my dear friends—life is so endlessly tasty!

Quick and Easy Beef, Lamb and Pork

Meats are often a go-to for low-carb meals. They provide a complete, high-quality protein, as well as iron and vitamin B12. I always recommend opting for grass-fed meats and avoiding processed meats to get the optimal nutritional benefits.

In this chapter, I will show you how to create a variety of entrées with beef, lamb and pork that are low carb, easy and finished in under 30 minutes. No matter who you are cooking for, you can rest assured that these dishes are packed with mouthwatering flavors that are sure to delight your taste buds, as well as impress everyone around the table. You will find everything from weeknight dinners to extravagant entrées fit for the biggest food connoisseurs or even your close family and friends. So, whip out your chef's hat and join me in the kitchen as we explore these versatile and flavorful meats.

Moroccan-Spiced Rack of Lamb with Curry Cauliflower Mash

Bring the wonderful taste of Morocco right into your home with this juicy and flavorful low-carb dish. It is so elegant and yet so quick and simple. The combination of ginger with cumin and coriander transforms the lamb into an earthy and mildly spiced delight. When paired with curry cauliflower, you get a fusion of tasty Moroccan and Indian cuisines. You'll feel good when you eat it, and you'll look like a pro when you plate it for the ones you love. Try purchasing fresh rack of lamb instead of frozen for a milder taste and to shop locally.

Serves 4

Moroccan-Spiced Lamb

1 tsp ground ginger

½ tsp cayenne pepper

½ tsp ground coriander

½ tsp ground cumin

1 tsp kosher salt

¼ tsp ground black pepper

1 lb (454 g) rack of lamb, frenched

3 tbsp (45 ml) extra virgin olive oil

1 cup (150 g) cherry tomatoes on the vine

Curry Cauliflower

3 cups (300 g) fresh or frozen cauliflower florets

⅔ cup (160 ml) bone broth or low-sodium beef broth

¾ tsp curry powder

2 tbsp (30 ml) nut milk or heavy cream

Kosher salt and ground black pepper

Preheat your oven to 425°F (220°C, or gas mark 7).

To make the lamb, mix the ginger, cayenne, coriander, cumin, salt and pepper in a small bowl. Lay your rack of lamb on a chopping board and score it on the surface by marking an "X" on the surface. This will make it easier for the insides to cook a lot quicker in the oven and for the lamb to absorb all of the wonderful flavors of the spices.

Generously rub the lamb all over with the spice mixture. Heat the oil in a large ovenproof skillet over medium-high heat. Cook the lamb until browned on both sides, about 5 minutes per side. You'll find that the ends of the rack are still a bit pink, which is fine. Add the tomatoes to the skillet. Using oven mitts, transfer the hot skillet to the oven. Bake for 12 to 15 minutes for medium-rare lamb.

In the meantime, make the curry cauliflower: Heat a medium-sized saucepan over medium-high heat. Add the cauliflower, broth, curry powder and nut milk. Season with salt and pepper, and bring to a boil for exactly 10 minutes. Use an immersion blender or transfer to a regular blender to puree, then set aside.

When your lamb is ready, take it out of the oven and let it rest. Always let your meat rest for 5 minutes so that all the juices are reabsorbed for a tender, juicier meat. Serve with the curry mash.

Chef's Notes: The cooking time for the lamb may vary depending on how you prefer it. If you like it well done, it may extend your prep and cooking time a little longer than 30 minutes.

Frenched rack of lamb is when rib bones are exposed by cutting off the fat and meat covering them. You can purchase your rack of lamb already frenched from the butcher.

Strip Loin Steak with Spicy Chili Chimichurri

Can you believe that something so simple can be so deliciously nutritious? Sometimes the best things come in minimal packaging—and that's exactly what this low-carb strip loin steak delivers with the extra spicy kick of the chili chimichurri sauce.

Serves 4

Strip Loin Steak

4 (8-oz [226-g]) strip loin steaks, ½ inch (1 cm) thick

Kosher salt and ground black pepper

1 (8-oz [226-g]) stick unsalted grass-fed butter, divided

Chili Chimichurri

1 chili pepper, chopped

2 cups (120 g) fresh parsley leaves

1 cup (16 g) fresh cilantro leaves

2–3 cloves garlic, minced

1 shallot, chopped

½ cup (120 ml) extra virgin olive oil

⅓ cup (80 ml) red wine vinegar

1 tsp kosher salt

¼ tsp ground black pepper

3 cups (340 g) cooked cauliflower rice, for serving (optional)

Leave your steaks at room temperature for about 5 to 8 minutes, then season with salt and pepper on both sides. Heat a 12-inch (30-cm) cast-iron skillet over high heat. Add half of the butter to the hot skillet. Right before it fizzles out, immediately drop in 2 steaks. Sear for about 3 minutes without moving to form a crust, then flip and cook the reverse side for 2 to 3 minutes. Add additional time if using thicker cuts. Transfer your steaks to a chopping board to rest for 5 to 10 minutes to absorb all those flavorful juices. Repeat the process by adding the remaining butter, then the remaining steaks.

To make the chimichurri: In a large food processor, add the chili pepper, parsley, cilantro, garlic, shallot, oil, vinegar, salt and pepper. Puree until smooth. Taste your sauce; the trick to really good chimichurri is in the garlic, and I believe the amount I've listed in this recipe is perfect, because it's been given a five-star review in my kitchen!

Slice your steak and spread about 2 tablespoons (30 ml) of chimichurri sauce on top. Serve with cauliflower rice (if using).

Zesty Mint Lettuce Lamb Burgers

"This heavenly, satisfying burger is one of the many reasons I look forward to eating dinner at your house."
A true quote from my dear mother, who is also happy being my guinea pig whenever
I'm testing meat recipes. These juicy, hot off the grill, low-carb lamb burgers will have
your mouth watering before they even hit your plate.

Serves 4

Lamb Burgers

1 lb (454 g) ground lamb

3 cloves garlic, minced

1 tbsp (6 g) chopped mint leaves

1 shallot, minced

Juice of 1 lime

½ tsp kosher salt

¼ tsp ground black pepper

For Serving

1 head butter lettuce

Sliced red peppers

Sliced red onions

2 cups (400 g) store-bought zucchini chips (optional)

To make the burgers, fire up the grill or grill pan to medium heat. I used a grill pan for this recipe. While the grill pan is heating up, mix the ground lamb with garlic, mint, shallot, lime juice, salt and pepper. Form 4 equal-sized lamb patties. Now comes the fun step: Grill the lamb burgers for approximately 4 minutes per side, making sure to only turn them once. You can also enjoy listening to the lovely sizzle in the pan while these burgers are cooking.

When the burgers are ready, it's building time. Layer the lamb burgers on the lettuce leaves with red peppers and onions. Serve with zucchini chips, if desired.

Stuffed Banana Peppers with Korean Ground Beef

They're light, filling and super quick to make—and will give you a kick in the pants! These spicy babies pack quite a punch, but they have made it onto the low-carb menu because of their uniquely flavorful appeal to the palate. You won't want to put them down once you pick them up. These are great with a tall glass of iced coconut water if you have any around.

Serves 4

16 hot banana peppers

¼ cup (60 ml) coconut aminos

½ tsp kosher salt

2 tsp (10 ml) sesame oil

¼ tsp ground ginger

3 cloves garlic, minced

2 lb (907 g) ground grass-fed beef

Olive oil, for grilling

3 cups (340 g) cooked cauliflower rice, for serving (optional)

Banana peppers are quite hot. I recommend you wear food-safe gloves, but it's not mandatory. If you choose not to use gloves, make sure you wash your hands with soap and water immediately after handling the peppers. Rinse the banana peppers. Carefully remove the tops and seeds, and set the seeds aside.

In a small bowl, whisk together 1 tablespoon (2 g) of the reserved pepper seeds, the coconut aminos, salt, sesame oil and ginger. Set aside.

In a 12-inch (30-cm) skillet over medium-high heat, cook the garlic and the ground beef until you no longer see pink, about 2 to 4 minutes. Pour in the coconut aminos mixture and let it simmer for about 2 minutes. Set aside when ready and allow to cool.

To grill and stuff the banana peppers, preheat your grill pan over medium-high heat. Carefully stuff the peppers with the ground beef. Stuff in as much beef as you can, so you get enough at the bottom.

Grease the grill pan lightly with a bit of oil. Grill both sides of the peppers for about 6 minutes until you get a nice smoky char. It's okay if you get a few pieces of ground beef falling out of the peppers. Serve with cauliflower rice (if using).

Spicy Salsa Verde Pork Chops

My dad used to look forward to pork chops for dinner when he came home after a long day at the office. Sometimes he would even leave work early if he knew my mom was making them. My quick and easy rendition with salsa verde is a spicy, low-carb delight you're going to look forward to on any weeknight.

Serves 4

Pork Chops

3 tbsp (45 ml) extra virgin olive oil

½ tsp kosher salt

¼ tsp ground black pepper

½ tsp garlic powder

¼ tsp onion powder

½ tsp chili powder

4 (8-oz [226-g]) pork loin chops, ½ inch (1 cm) thick

Salsa Verde

1 cup (16 g) fresh cilantro leaves

½ cup (46 g) fresh mint leaves

1 tbsp (9 g) capers

Juice of 1 lime

1 tsp white wine vinegar

1½ tbsp (23 ml) honey Dijon mustard

2–3 mini pickles or 1 regular-sized kosher dill pickle

Spring mix salad, for serving

Preheat your oven to 400°F (200°C, or gas mark 6). Line a sheet pan with parchment paper.

To make the pork chops: In a small bowl, combine the oil, salt, pepper, garlic powder, onion powder and chili powder. Lay the pork chops on the sheet pan. Use a basting brush or your hands to coat both sides of the pork chops with the seasoning mixture.

Bake the pork chops for approximately 15 minutes, then let them rest on the counter for 5 minutes. Add additional time for thicker cuts.

To make the salsa, pulse the cilantro, mint, capers, lime juice, vinegar, Dijon mustard and pickles in a food processor until smooth.

Top the pork chops with the salsa verde, and serve with the spring mix salad.

Chef's Notes: If you have pickles that already contain garlic, cut the garlic powder down to ⅛ teaspoon.

The leftover salsa verde stays fresh in the fridge for up to 2 days.

Rosemary Balsamic Lamb Chops with Roasted Veggies

Lamb chops are a very tender cut of meat and, when done right, they can make a super flavorful and aromatic weeknight dinner. These 30-minute, oven-baked, low-carb lamb chops take your dining experience to the next level with the lovely hints of rosemary and olive oil and the mild smokiness of the roasted veggies.

Serves 6

6 (8-oz [226-g]) lamb loin chops

½ cup plus 2 tbsp (150 ml) extra virgin olive oil, divided

1 tsp kosher salt, plus more for seasoning

¼ tsp black pepper, plus more for seasoning

1 tsp garlic powder

2 zucchinis, chopped

2 cups (200 g) chopped cauliflower florets

1 jalapeño or chili pepper

15 asparagus stalks, ends removed

1 tbsp (2 g) chopped fresh rosemary

3 tbsp (45 ml) unsweetened balsamic reduction

Preheat your oven to 400°F (200°C, or gas mark 6). Set the bottom rack at least two rows away from the top rack. Line a sheet pan with parchment paper.

Lay your lamb chops on a chopping board and drizzle with ¼ cup (60 ml) of the oil. In a small bowl, mix the salt, pepper and garlic powder and rub it into each loin.

Toss the zucchinis, cauliflower, jalapeño and asparagus on the sheet pan, then drizzle them with ¼ cup (60 ml) of the oil and season with salt and pepper.

Place an ovenproof skillet over medium-high heat and add the remaining 2 tablespoons (30 ml) of oil. Brown the lamb chops for 2 to 3 minutes per side, until golden brown. When done, top with the rosemary and transfer to the oven on the top rack. Place the veggies on the bottom rack. Bake the lamb for 15 minutes for medium-rare or 20 minutes for well done. Bake the veggies for 20 minutes.

Drizzle the lamb with balsamic reduction or serve on the side.

Chef's Note: You can purchase organic balsamic glaze/reduction. Just be sure to look for one that is unsweetened. If you prefer to make your own, see the Chef's Note on page 104, but be aware this may up the cook time to over 30 minutes.

Marinated Skirt Steak with Manchego Vinaigrette

Sometimes the best way to get the most wonderful flavors out of your steak is through great marinades. For this skirt steak, you can prep the marinade overnight so you'll be guaranteed an even quicker delicious low-carb dinner. Paired with the earthiness of radicchio, this steak is the perfect way to bring the dining experience into your home.

Serves 2

Marinated Skirt Steak

¼ cup (60 ml) coconut aminos

1 tbsp (15 ml) rice vinegar

¼ cup (60 ml) extra virgin olive oil

1 tsp dried thyme

1 tsp dried parsley

½ tsp ground black pepper

1 tsp kosher salt

½ tsp garlic powder

¼ tsp ground ginger

1 lb (454 g) skirt steak

Manchego Vinaigrette

¼ cup (60 ml) balsamic vinegar

¼ cup (60 ml) flaxseed oil

1 shallot, chopped

1 tbsp (15 ml) monk fruit syrup

Kosher salt and ground black pepper

4 oz (113 g) Manchego cheese, shredded

1 head of radicchio halved, cored and chopped into 1-inch (2.5-cm) pieces

To get the best out of this recipe, marinate the steak overnight. In a large ziplock bag, combine the coconut aminos, vinegar, oil, thyme, parsley, pepper, salt, garlic powder and ginger. Add the skirt steak, making sure the steak is coated well. Refrigerate overnight.

Before cooking, leave the steak out of the fridge for 10 minutes. Place a 12-inch (30-cm) cast-iron skillet over medium-high heat. You do not have to grease your pan; the marinade already contains olive oil. Remove your steak from the marinade. Sear the steak for 3 minutes per side, then let it rest for 10 minutes.

To make the vinaigrette: Use a glass bowl with a whisk, a dressing shaker or even a martini shaker. Combine the balsamic vinegar, flaxseed oil, shallot and monk fruit syrup. Season to taste with salt and pepper. Stir in the Manchego cheese.

Toss the radicchio with the dressing until it's coated all over. Slice your skirt steak and serve with the salad.

Chef's Notes: You can use flank steak for this recipe if you cannot find skirt steak.

You can also find monk fruit syrup online or at organic stores. It's refined sugar–free and low-glycemic.

Wine and Garlic Pork Chops with Crispy Asparagus

For those evenings when you have unexpected company, never fear. Inspired by one of my favorite Food Network chefs, my low-carb version of wine and garlic pork chops serves up a flavorful punch with dry red wine, aromatic garlic and a side of crispy asparagus. It's healthy and yummy—and it's all accomplished in under 30 minutes.

Serves 4

Pork Chops

4 bone-in T-bone pork chops, 1 inch (2.5 cm) thick

Kosher salt and ground black pepper

2 tbsp (30 ml) extra virgin olive oil

2 tbsp (28 g) unsalted grass-fed butter

8 cloves garlic, peeled and lightly smashed

1½ cups (360 ml) dry red wine

1 bay leaf

½ cup (120 ml) low-sodium beef broth

1 tbsp (15 ml) balsamic vinegar

Crispy Asparagus

2 tbsp (28 g) unsalted grass-fed butter

12 asparagus stalks, ends chopped

Dash of kosher salt

Season both sides of the pork chops with salt and pepper. Heat the oil and butter in a 12-inch (30-cm) cast-iron skillet over high heat. Lightly brown the pork chops in the skillet for 1 minute per side, but don't cook them all the way through. Remove the pork chops and set them aside on a plate.

Reduce the heat to medium-high and throw in the whole cloves of garlic. Keep stirring the garlic until it gets golden brown. Pour in the red wine, then add the bay leaf and stir it around and cook. Keep stirring until the sauce is reduced and thick, at least 3 to 5 minutes.

Stir in the broth and add the pork chops back into the skillet. Cook the chops in the skillet for about 3 minutes, then add the balsamic vinegar. Shake the skillet to get it to distribute, then cook for 3 minutes, or until a meat thermometer reaches 145°F (63°C).

Remove the pork chops from the skillet. Let the sauce reduce for about a minute, allowing the sauce to thicken and the garlic to soften. Discard the bay leaf, then pour the sauce on the pork chops.

To make the asparagus: Heat a saucepan over medium-high heat with the butter and sprinkle the asparagus with a dash of salt. Toast the asparagus until browned, about 2 minutes, shaking the pan to ensure that the asparagus is coated.

Chef's Note: The best way to quickly peel a whole garlic clove is to gently smash it with a chef's knife. That way the skin falls off easily. Alternatively, you can also purchase peeled garlic from the grocery store.

Summer Steak Salad with Gorgonzola

I got inspired to make this salad on a summer evening after I got home from a picnic and didn't know what to do with my leftover Gorgonzola. I fried up some New York strip steaks I had in the fridge. Then I threw together an arugula salad with some juicy cherry tomatoes picked from my garden and finished it all off with a simple olive oil–balsamic vinaigrette. My partner went from a hungry hippo to a happy hubby. That's how good this salad is.

Serves 4

Steak

4 (1-lb [454-g]) New York strip steaks, ½ inch (1 cm) thick

Kosher salt and ground black pepper

3 tbsp (45 ml) extra virgin olive oil

¼ cup (57 g) unsalted grass-fed butter

Salad

12 cups (240 g) baby arugula

⅔ cup (80 g) crumbled Gorgonzola

2 cups (300 g) cherry tomatoes, halved

2 tbsp (30 ml) balsamic vinegar

2 tbsp (30 ml) extra virgin olive oil

Season the steaks with salt and pepper. Coat a 12-inch (30-cm) cast-iron skillet with the oil and heat it over high heat. Quickly add the steaks to the hot pan and cook for 3 minutes. Flip the steaks, add the butter, then swirl the butter around the steaks and cook for 2 to 3 minutes. Remove the steaks from the pan and let them rest for 10 minutes while you make your salad.

To make the salad: In a large bowl, toss the arugula, Gorgonzola, tomatoes, vinegar and oil until combined.

Cut the steaks diagonally across the grain into thin slices. Serve the salad with the steak on top.

Beef Tenderloin and Shiitake Mushroom, Chipotle Butter and Tomberry

This is a quick dinner that is as fancy as it sounds, but not intimidating to put together. The juicy beef tenderloin and mushrooms, combined with a light creaminess and the spicy chipotle, are finished off with a little sweetness from the Tomberry. You will definitely be giving your kitchen a few Michelin stars.

Serves 4

Mushroom and Tomberry Sauté

2 tbsp (28 g) unsalted grass-fed butter, at room temperature

1–2 tsp (3–6 g) finely chopped chipotle chile in adobo sauce

2 tbsp (30 ml) extra virgin olive oil

1 shallot, chopped

2 cloves garlic, minced

3–4 cups (210–280 g) shiitake mushrooms, stems removed and chopped

1 cup (100 g) Tomberry® tomatoes

⅓ cup (80 ml) dry white wine

¼ tsp ground black pepper

⅛ tsp kosher salt

Beef Tenderloin

2 tbsp (30 ml) extra virgin olive oil

4 (4-oz [113-g]) beef tenderloin steaks, 1 inch (2.5 cm) thick

½ tsp kosher salt

½ tsp ground black pepper

To make the sauté, mix the butter and chipotle in a small bowl. Set aside.

Heat a saucepan over medium-high heat. Add the oil and sauté the shallot, garlic, mushrooms and tomatoes for about 5 minutes. While stirring, add the wine and cook for 2 minutes or until the liquid almost evaporates, scraping the pan to loosen any browned bits. Stir in the pepper and salt, then remove the pan from the heat. Add 1 tablespoon (15 ml) of the chipotle butter and stir until the mushrooms and Tomberry tomatoes are coated. Set aside.

To make the beef tenderloin: Don't turn off your burner; just switch your saucepan to a 12-inch (30-cm) cast-iron skillet. Coat the skillet with oil. Season both sides of the steaks with the salt and pepper and add the steaks to the pan, then cook 4 minutes per side for medium rare. Remove the steaks from the pan and top them with the remaining chipotle butter. Serve with the shiitake mushrooms and Tomberry sauté.

> Chef's Note: Tomberry tomatoes are basically little tomatoes. If you can't find them, cherry tomatoes will work just fine.

Hungarian-Inspired Pork Paprikash with Spiralized Zucchini

This twist on a Hungarian classic comes together with all the delicious delights you love about pork and the efficiency that comes with low-carb cooking. The paprika really shines in this dish— if you couldn't tell from the title that it was trying to show off just a little. It's mildly spicy and perfectly nutty with hints of almond meal, and the spiralized zucchini adds a nice bite of sweetness and freshness to cleanse the palate. This is one of those perfect lazy-proof recipes you can whip up so easily: prepped, cooked and served in under 30 minutes.

Serves 6

Pork Paprikash

1 lb (454 g) pork tenderloin, trimmed and cut into 1-inch (2.5-cm) cubes

2 tbsp (12 g) almond meal

1 tbsp (7 g) paprika

¼ tsp ground black pepper

¼ tsp cayenne pepper

2 tbsp (30 ml) extra virgin olive oil

2 (14.5-oz [411-g]) cans fire-roasted diced tomatoes (no salt added)

1 (8-oz [226-g]) can tomato sauce

1 medium red bell pepper, cut into thin strips

¼ tsp kosher salt (optional)

Spiralized Zucchini

2 tsp (10 ml) extra virgin olive oil

3–4 zucchinis, spiralized

1 tsp kosher salt

For Serving

½ cup (120 ml) crème fraîche or sour cream

1 bunch fresh parsley, chopped

In a large ziplock bag, add the pork, almond meal, paprika, pepper and cayenne. Shake the bag until the pork is tossed in the almond meal mixture. Heat the oil in a 12-inch (30-cm) skillet over medium-high heat and add the pork. Cook for 5 minutes until brown.

While the pork is still in the skillet, add the tomatoes, tomato sauce, bell pepper and salt (if using). Stir to combine, then bring to a simmer and reduce the heat slightly. Cover the skillet and simmer for 10 minutes.

To make the zucchini, heat another skillet over medium-high heat with 2 teaspoons (10 ml) of oil. Cook the zucchini for 3 to 5 minutes, adding the salt 1 minute into cooking. Stir constantly, then transfer to a serving dish. Discard the zucchini liquid from the pan.

Serve the zucchini with the Hungarian paprikash, a dollop of crème fraîche and some parsley.

Thyme Rib Eye Steak with Cauliflower Rice

A perfect, easy rib eye steak paired with flavorful cauliflower rice to make your weeknight low-carb cooking a breeze. It's butter-basted with fresh thyme, perfectly juicy and—of course— very quick to make. I call this dish the steak and bake.

Serves 4

Thyme Rib Eye Steak

4 (16-oz [454-g]) rib eye steaks, 1½ inches (4 cm) thick

1 tsp kosher salt

½ tsp coarse ground black pepper

¼ cup (57 g) unsalted grass-fed butter

6 sprigs of fresh thyme

Cauliflower Rice

2 tbsp (30 ml) extra virgin olive oil

4 cups (453 g) store-bought cauliflower rice

1 tsp onion powder

½ tsp kosher salt

¼ tsp ground black pepper

Preheat your oven to 500°F (260°C, or gas mark 10). Heat a cast-iron skillet over high heat. Use caution; the pan will be very hot.

Season the steaks with the salt and pepper, then add the butter to the pan and add the steaks. Sear the steaks on high heat for about 30 seconds on each side, just until lightly browned, then top the steaks with the thyme sprigs and spoon the butter onto the steaks.

Put the steaks in the oven for 7 to 9 minutes. Then when ready, remove them from the oven and let them rest for 5 minutes before cutting.

To make the cauliflower rice, place another skillet over medium-high heat and add the oil. Add the cauliflower rice, onion powder, salt and pepper. Keep stirring until the cauliflower starts to soften up a little bit, about 2 to 4 minutes.

Serve the steak with the cauliflower rice on the side.

Skillet Pork Loin, Asparagus and Peaches

It only takes a few ingredients to make this meal a delicious, quick and simple delight. It's low carb and uniquely paired with the asparagus and peaches. It's like a marriage that your in-laws may have been skeptical about in the beginning, but it all worked out perfectly in the end.

Serves 4

1½ lb (680 g) boneless pork loin

Kosher salt and ground black pepper

¼ cup (60 ml) coconut aminos

1 tbsp (15 ml) hot sauce

2 tbsp (30 ml) avocado oil

12–15 asparagus stalks, chopped with stems removed

3 firm peaches, pitted and sliced

½ cup (120 ml) dry Marsala wine

¼ cup (10 g) chopped basil

Slice your pork loin about ½ inch (1 cm) thick, then sprinkle lightly with salt and pepper. In a small ramekin, combine the coconut aminos and hot sauce. You can also brush a little bit of the coconut aminos mixture on the sliced pork loins for added flavor.

Place a 12-inch (30-cm) skillet over medium-high heat. Add the oil and brown the pork loin on both sides for about 1 minute on each side. Transfer the pork to a dish, but keep it covered. You want to keep it warm because you are not quite done cooking it yet.

Add the asparagus and peaches to the skillet, stirring occasionally for about 5 minutes until the asparagus starts to brown and the peaches start to caramelize a little. Sprinkle with a dash more salt and pepper. Add the coconut aminos mixture and Marsala wine to the skillet, then return the pork to the skillet and cook for 5 minutes just until done. Flip the pork, then transfer the pork, asparagus and peaches to a serving platter. Continue to boil the sauce gently until slightly thickened, about 2 to 3 minutes. Pour the sauce over the pork, top with basil and serve.

Chef's Note: Use coconut aminos as a soy- and sodium-free substitute for soy sauce. You can find coconut aminos at natural food stores or online.

Italian-Style Meatballs

You know that expression, "just like mama used to make"? Well, although I'm a believer that nothing tastes exactly like mama's good cooking, these low-carb Italian-style meatballs are pretty close—and they come together in under 30 minutes. The fusion of beef and pork creates a delicious flavor profile, and the marinara gives extra moisture and sauciness, which brings it close to home and even closer to your mama's approval.

Serves 4

½ lb (226 g) ground grass-fed beef

½ lb (226 g) ground pork

¼ cup (60 ml) half-and-half

1 large egg, beaten

¼ tsp onion powder

¼ tsp dried oregano

¼ tsp dried basil

1 clove garlic, minced

½ tsp kosher salt

¼ tsp ground black pepper

¼ cup (25 g) freshly grated Parmesan cheese

¾–1 cup (180–240 ml) store-bought organic marinara sauce

¼ cup (28 g) shredded mozzarella cheese

½ cup (30 g) chopped fresh Italian parsley, for serving

2 (14-oz [397-g]) cans cooked palmini linguine, for serving (optional)

Preheat your oven to 400°F (200°C, or gas mark 6). Grease an ovenproof 10- to 12-inch (26- to 30-cm) Pyrex or baking dish.

In a large bowl, combine the beef, pork, half-and-half, egg, onion powder, oregano, basil, garlic, salt, pepper and Parmesan. Do not overmix or it will become too mushy.

Divide the mixture into 12 to 14 balls; you may get more or less depending on how big or small you make the balls. Keep in mind that if your meatballs are on the larger side, it will lengthen your baking time.

Place the meatballs in the baking dish and transfer to the oven. Bake for 20 minutes. Around the 15-minute mark, take out the meatballs and top with marinara sauce and mozzarella, then return to the oven for the remaining 5 minutes.

Top with parsley and serve with the palmini (if using).

Chef's Notes: Palmini is a low-carb pasta substitute, made completely out of a natural plant known as hearts of palm. See page 120 for cooking instructions. Palmini should be soaked in milk overnight and rinsed, then boiled for 10 minutes.

These meatballs can be stored for up to 5 days in an airtight container.

Apple-Onion Pork Tenderloin

When it comes to pork, there's no better combination than apple and onion. It creates a perfect combination of sweetness and tartness with just the right amount of acidity. You really can't go wrong with this fail-proof, weeknight, low-carb pork tenderloin.

Serves 4

2 tbsp (30 ml) avocado oil, divided

1 lb (454 g) pork tenderloin, cut in half

3 tbsp (45 ml) maple mustard

2 medium red apples, thinly sliced

1 medium red onion, halved and thinly sliced

½ cup (120 ml) raw apple cider vinegar

¼ tsp kosher salt

¼ tsp ground white pepper

Preheat your oven to 425°F (220°C, or gas mark 7).

Place a 12-inch (30-cm) skillet over medium-high heat and add 1 tablespoon (15 ml) of avocado oil. Brown the pork for about 45 seconds per side, then remove the pan from the heat. Use a spoon and spread maple mustard on top of the pork, then transfer to the oven and bake for 15 to 18 minutes.

Place another skillet over medium-high heat. Add the remaining avocado oil, apples and onion. Stir in the vinegar and bring to a boil, then stir in salt and pepper. Reduce the heat and simmer for about 5 minutes until nice and slightly tender. By this time, the pork should be about done, so take it out of the oven and let it rest for a couple of minutes before slicing. Serve with the apple-and-onion mixture.

Mediterranean Romaine Steak Tacos

My love for tacos and Mediterranean food became even more intensified with the combination
of this juicy New York strip steak and flavorful Mediterranean olives, cherry tomatoes and a dash of
rosemary. It's all about smart combinations to make this meal a delicious success.
Plus, it's quick, easy and ready in under 30 minutes.

Serves 4

4 (6-oz [170-g]) New York strip steaks,
1 inch (2.5 cm) thick

½ tsp kosher salt

¼ tsp ground black pepper

2 tsp (1 g) dried rosemary, crushed

2 tbsp (30 ml) Greek or extra virgin
olive oil, divided

2 cloves garlic, minced

2 cups (300 g) cherry tomatoes, halved

½ cup (90 g) pitted Kalamata olives,
chopped

1 tsp lemon zest

4 romaine lettuce leaves

1 lemon, cut into 4 wedges

Season your steaks with salt, pepper and rosemary by rubbing both sides. Place a
12-inch (30-cm) cast-iron skillet over medium-high heat and add 1 tablespoon
(15 ml) of oil. Sear the steaks for 4 minutes per side for medium-rare, then remove
the steaks from the skillet and keep warm. If using thicker steaks, add additional
time.

Add the remaining tablespoon (15 ml) of oil to the same skillet. Sauté the garlic
and tomatoes for 1 to 2 minutes until fragrant and the tomatoes begin to wrinkle.
Turn the heat off and stir in the olives and lemon zest, while giving it a gentle toss.

Top the romaine leaves with sliced steak and the tomato mixture, and serve with
lemon wedges on the side.

Steak au Poivre

Sometimes all you need is pepper cream, especially on steak. My mother had a variation of this dish on one of her trips to Paris and she loved it, so I decided to create this low-carb, quick and easy version, which she loved even more. The cracked black peppercorns and hints of Grand Marnier blend so perfectly with the cream, which adds a delightful flavor component to the steak.

Serves 4

1–2 tbsp (5–10 g) cracked peppercorns

4 (14-oz [397-g]) beef tenderloin steaks, cut 1 inch (2.5 cm) thick

2 tbsp (28 g) grass-fed butter

¼ cup (60 ml) beef broth

¼ cup (60 ml) Grand Marnier or brandy

½ cup (120 ml) heavy cream

2 tsp (10 ml) Dijon mustard

3 cups (340 g) cooked cauliflower rice, for serving (optional)

Generously rub the cracked peppercorns on the steaks. Place a 12-inch (30-cm) skillet over medium heat and add the butter. Add the steaks to the skillet and cook for 18 minutes for medium-rare, turning only once, 9 minutes per side. Tenderloin cuts are very thick and need time to cook on medium heat. Transfer the steaks to a serving platter and reserve the drippings in the skillet.

Add the broth and Grand Marnier carefully into the drippings in the skillet, scraping up the lovely crusty browned bits. You will get a nice whiff of the orange liqueur. Stir in the heavy cream and Dijon mustard. Turn up the heat slightly and bring to a boil, uncovered, then reduce the heat again to medium for about 2 to 3 minutes. By then, the mixture should be reduced to about ½ cup (120 ml). Stir the sauce to avoid burning.

Spoon the sauce over the steaks and serve with cauliflower rice (if using). Let your mind escape to France for a few minutes.

Antipasto Salad with Olive Oil and White Wine Dressing

This antipasto brings all the things you love about a charcuterie board and incorporates it in a low-carb version of a hearty salad with the addition of crispy bacon. It's healthy, fresh and so quick to put together. Make it after a long day at work or when you get back from the gym.

Serves 4

Salad

5 cups (275 g) chopped butter lettuce

10 cooked bacon strips, chopped

½ cup (66 g) cubed aged Cheddar

½ cup (56 g) cubed mozzarella

½ cup (27 g) sugar-free sun-dried tomatoes, sliced

¼ cup (40 g) sliced black olives

¼ cup (10 g) chopped fresh basil

Olive Oil and White Wine Dressing

⅓ cup (80 ml) extra virgin olive oil

2 tbsp (30 ml) white wine vinegar

1 small shallot, minced

½ tsp maple Dijon mustard

Kosher salt and ground black pepper

To make the salad, add the lettuce, bacon, Cheddar, mozzarella, sun-dried tomatoes, olives and basil to a large bowl.

To make the dressing: In a food processor or a dressing shaker, combine the oil, vinegar, shallot, mustard and salt and pepper to taste.

Pour the dressing over the salad and toss until coated. You're ready to eat!

Simple and Delicious Poultry

Poultry is also a healthy option for low-carb meals because it is a lighter alternative to other meats. It's also easy to prep for a quick weeknight dinner. And turkey and chicken are great sources of lean protein, which contributes to muscle growth and development.

In this chapter, I will take you on a delicious tour of my kitchen featuring low-carb poultry dishes such as my elegant Rosemary and White Wine Chicken (page 54) and the flavorful spices in my Cajun Portobello Chicken Burgers (page 50). These dishes are sure to satisfy your cravings, and they can be made start-to-finish in under 30 minutes. Get your herbs and your chef's knives ready! Cooking class is now in session.

Red Curry Turkey Meatballs with Thai Peanut Sauce

Inspired by my trip to Thailand, these red curry turkey meatballs scream great flavor. With a delicious combination of spicy, sweet and sour hints from the curry and peanut sauce, it's no wonder Thai cuisine is so popular. It's low carb and elegant, and it comes together in no time.

Serves 6

Turkey Meatballs

1 lb (454 g) ground turkey

1 tbsp (8 g) garlic powder

1 tbsp (15 ml) Thai fish sauce

1 egg

½ tsp onion powder

½ tsp dried thyme

¼ tsp paprika

½ tsp kosher salt

½ tsp ground black pepper

1 cup (104 g) almond flour

Peanut Sauce

1 tbsp (15 ml) extra virgin olive oil

1 (14-oz [414-ml]) can full-fat coconut milk

1 tbsp (14 g) red curry paste

2 tbsp (32 g) organic peanut butter

¼ tsp cayenne pepper

Kosher salt and ground black pepper

For Serving

½ cup (8 g) chopped fresh cilantro

5 cups (425 g) cooked zoodles (optional)

Preheat your oven to 375°F (190°C, or gas mark 5). Line a baking sheet with parchment paper or a silicone ovenproof mat, and set it aside.

In a large bowl, combine the turkey, garlic powder, fish sauce, egg, onion powder, thyme, paprika, salt, pepper and almond flour. Form medium-sized balls and place them on the lined baking sheet. The balls should be about the size of a cookie scoop, so roughly ½ inch (1 cm) thick; you should end up with about 20 to 22 meatballs. Place the turkey meatballs in the oven and bake for 20 to 25 minutes. The smaller your turkey meatballs are, the quicker they will bake.

To make the Thai peanut sauce: Heat the oil in a medium-sized saucepan over medium-high heat. Add the coconut milk, curry paste, peanut butter, cayenne pepper and salt and pepper to taste. Bring to a boil. Reduce the heat to medium-low and let it simmer for 5 minutes. Turn the heat off.

When your turkey meatballs are ready, transfer them to a large serving bowl. Pour the peanut sauce over the turkey meatballs until they are evenly coated. Use a fork or tongs to move the meatballs around a little bit to get them to absorb the sauce. Top with cilantro and serve with zoodles (if using).

Cajun Portobello Chicken Burgers

These are definitely one of my favorite creations, simply because of my love for Cajun-flavored anything and everything. Cajun spice and jalapeños were all I needed to make this low-carb, juicy chicken burger a delicious hit. No need for bread crumbs or added flours—just simple flavorful ingredients that will take you less than 30 minutes to prep, grill and eat.

Serves 4

1 lb (454 g) ground chicken

1 tsp Cajun spice, organic store-bought or homemade

2 cloves garlic, minced

1 medium shallot, minced

1 jalapeño pepper, thinly chopped

4 portobello mushroom caps, stems removed and insides cleaned

1 tbsp (15 ml) olive oil, for brushing

Olive oil spray, for the grill pan

Lettuce, for serving

Sliced tomatoes, for serving

In a large bowl, combine the chicken, Cajun spice, garlic, shallot and jalapeño pepper. Your mixture might be a bit mushy, which is fine; don't overmix because you want a little bit of elasticity to form patties. Brush the insides of your portobello mushroom caps with a little bit of oil. Set them aside.

Place a grill pan over medium heat and spray it with oil. Form patties about ½ inch (1 cm) thick and place them on the grill pan. Grill both sides for 10 to 12 minutes.

When the patties are done, grill the mushrooms in the pan for about 4 minutes per side. There will be no need to grease the pan as the mushrooms have quite a bit of moisture in them.

When ready, assemble your burgers on grilled portobello mushrooms with your lettuce and tomato toppings.

Spicy Chicken Popper Fritters

This recipe is basically everything you love about jalapeño poppers made into a fritter—with added chicken, so there's even more to love. It's yummy and spicy low-carb goals to win weeknight dinners every single night of the week.

Serves 4

Fritters

1 cup (112 g) shredded mozzarella cheese

2 jalapeño peppers, finely diced

2 shallots, finely diced

2 pieces boneless, skinless chicken breast, finely diced (1½ lb [680 g] total)

2 eggs

⅓ cup (37 g) coconut flour

½ tsp garlic powder

½ tsp dried oregano

Kosher salt and ground black pepper

1 tbsp (15 ml) extra virgin olive oil, for frying

For Serving

1 tbsp (15 ml) olive oil

1 tbsp (15 ml) balsamic vinegar

4 cups (120 g) baby arugula

Aioli

Aioli

¾ cup (172 g) mayonnaise

3 cloves garlic, minced

2 tbsp (30 ml) lime juice

½ tsp kosher salt

¼ tsp ground black pepper

To make the fritters: Combine the cheese, jalapeño peppers, shallots and chicken in a large bowl. Add the eggs, coconut flour, garlic powder, oregano, salt and pepper. Mix until combined.

Heat a 12-inch (30-cm) nonstick skillet over medium heat and add the oil. Using a ¼-cup (60-ml) measure, lightly grease the measuring cup and scoop out the fritter mixture into the skillet, making sure to flatten out the fritter. Repeat the process until the batter is used up or almost used up depending on how big your skillet is. Be careful not to crowd the pan; you don't want the fritters to touch. Fry until golden brown on both sides, about 6 to 8 minutes. Be sure to regulate the temperature so that they do not burn.

To serve, combine the oil and vinegar in a small bowl. Add the arugula to a large bowl and toss with the dressing. Mix the aioli ingredients in a bowl. Serve the fritters hot with aioli for dipping and a side of arugula salad.

Rosemary and White Wine Chicken

There is something so elegant about cooking with rosemary and wine. Whether they are used as a flavor enhancer or as a garnish, the combination of these ingredients always adds a unique touch to your food. Served alongside chopped zucchini, this quick, low-carb rosemary and white wine chicken entrée is always one to please.

Serves 4

4 boneless, skinless chicken breasts (1¾ lb [794 g] total)

1½ tbsp (23 ml) extra virgin olive oil, divided

1 tsp kosher salt, plus more for seasoning

Ground black pepper

2 cloves garlic, minced

2 tsp (1 g) fresh rosemary, minced

3 large zucchinis, chopped

⅓ cup (80 ml) dry white wine

Preheat your oven to 400°F (200°C, or gas mark 6) and be sure there is a rack at the bottom. Line 2 baking sheets with parchment paper.

Rub the chicken breasts with 1 tablespoon (15 ml) of oil, and sprinkle with salt and pepper. Rub the garlic and rosemary into the chicken breasts. Set aside.

Place the zucchini and chicken separately on the lined baking sheets. Sprinkle the zucchini with 1 teaspoon of salt and drizzle with the remaining olive oil. Place the chicken and zucchini in the oven with the zucchini on the bottom rack. Bake for 20 minutes.

When you remove the chicken from the oven, transfer to a serving platter, then immediately pour the white wine over it, serve with zucchini and enjoy.

Creamy Chicken Marsala

Did someone say chicken Marsala? Yup, you definitely heard that right. There's nothing more wonderful to look forward to on a weeknight than a quick skillet of low-carb, creamy chicken sizzling in garlic and mushrooms and soaking up the flavors of Marsala wine. I guess the only other thing to look forward to is having this dish already waiting for you when you get home.

Serves 4

4 boneless, skinless chicken breasts (2 lb [907 g] total)

4 tbsp (30 g) coconut flour

Kosher salt and ground black pepper

2 tbsp (30 ml) grapeseed oil

4 oz (113 g) sliced shiitake mushrooms, stems removed

2 cloves garlic, minced

1 shallot, chopped

1 cup (240 ml) organic chicken broth

½ cup (120 ml) dry Marsala wine

¾ cup (180 ml) heavy cream

½ cup (30 g) chopped fresh Italian parsley

2 (14-oz [397-g]) cans cooked palmini or 3 cups (340 g) cooked cauliflower rice (optional)

Dredge your chicken in the coconut flour until coated, then season both sides with salt and pepper. Be cautious not to over-season the chicken with too much salt; the Marsala wine and broth will be your main seasoning ingredients.

Heat a 12-inch (30-cm) nonstick skillet over medium heat and add the grapeseed oil. Sauté the mushrooms, garlic and shallot until soft, about 2 to 3 minutes. Add the chicken breasts and sear for about 5 minutes per side. Once browned, add the broth and Marsala wine. Simmer to reduce, then allow the chicken to cook for about 3 minutes. Add the heavy cream to finish the sauce and cook for 1 minute.

Season with additional salt and pepper, if desired. Turn the heat off and top the chicken with parsley. Serve with palmini or cauliflower rice (if using).

Chef's Note: If using palmini, simply follow the cooking instructions on the can. If you are not familiar with palmini, see page 120.

Crispy Lemon and Tomato Thyme Chicken Thighs

Who needs fast-food fried chicken when you can whip up these healthy and super delicious crispy chicken thighs in 30 minutes? With only six ingredients, this low-carb skillet chicken will soon become a crowd-pleaser . . . only if you choose to share.

Serves 4

4–5 bone-in, skin-on chicken thighs (1¾ lb [794 g] total)

2 tbsp (30 ml) extra virgin olive oil, divided

Kosher salt and ground black pepper

½ cup (75 g) cherry tomatoes on the vine

1 medium Meyer or regular lemon, thinly sliced

6 sprigs of fresh thyme

Steamed or roasted broccoli, for serving (optional)

Preheat your oven to 400°F (200°C, or gas mark 6). Arrange the rack right in the middle.

Rub the chicken thighs with 1 tablespoon (15 ml) oil, salt and pepper. I recommend you give them a generous rub for extra flavor.

Heat a 12-inch (30-cm) cast-iron skillet over medium heat and add the remaining oil. Cook your chicken thighs with the skin side down for 15 minutes, until the fat has rendered out. Turn the heat off, add the tomatoes and swirl around the rendered fat. Flip the chicken thighs so they are skin side up.

Scatter the lemon slices and thyme sprigs over the chicken and transfer the skillet to the oven. Roast for 18 minutes. Serve with steamed or roasted broccoli (if using).

Grilled Chili Chimichurri Chicken

Chimichurri is normally served as a spicy, flavorful green sauce over meats. It is also a favorite in this cookbook. I'm putting a slight spin on things by infusing the wonderful flavors of the chimichurri right in the chicken and slapping it on the grill. You're getting the spicy, smoky hints of garlic and an overall flavor explosion—all accomplished in 30 minutes.

Serves 4

1 chili pepper, chopped

2 cups (120 g) fresh parsley leaves

1 cup (16 g) fresh cilantro leaves

2–3 cloves garlic, minced

1 shallot, chopped

½ cup (120 ml) extra virgin olive oil

⅓ cup (80 ml) red wine vinegar

1 tsp kosher salt

¼ tsp ground pepper

4 bone-in, skin-on chicken thighs (1¾ lb [794 g] total)

Field greens, for serving (optional)

To make the chili chimichurri: Add the chili pepper, parsley, cilantro, garlic, shallot, oil, vinegar, salt and pepper to a food processor. Puree until semismooth.

Place the chicken thighs in a large bowl. Use a ⅓-cup (80-ml) measuring cup to add the chimichurri to the chicken. Toss to combine.

Place a grill pan over medium-high heat or set up an outdoor grill. Grill the chicken for 5 minutes per side. When it gets nice and browned, reduce the heat to medium-low and cover the grill pan or the grill. Let the chicken cook for 15 minutes until it's cooked all the way through. Serve with field greens (if using) and extra chimichurri for dipping.

Thai Chicken Green Curry

For those chilly fall or winter evenings when you're craving comfort food, whip up this quick pot of delicious Thai curry and get nice and cozy on the couch with a bowl in your hand. It will definitely be an evening well spent. The green curry paste offers the aromatic flavors of lemongrass, green chiles and makrut lime leaves. Thirty-minute cooking couldn't be more fabulous or indulgent.

Serves 6

2 boneless, skinless chicken breasts, sliced thin (1 lb [454 g] total)

½ tsp kosher salt

1 tbsp (14 g) organic coconut oil

2–3 shallots, chopped

1 chili pepper, thinly chopped and seeds removed

2 tbsp (28 g) Thai green curry paste

2 (14-oz [414-ml]) cans full-fat coconut milk

2 tbsp (30 ml) Thai fish sauce

3 cups (300 g) fresh or frozen cauliflower florets

1 red bell pepper, thinly sliced and seeds removed

Juice of 1 lime

¼ cup (4 g) chopped fresh cilantro leaves

Season your chicken breasts with salt. Heat the oil in a Dutch oven over medium heat. Add the shallots and chili pepper and cook until softened, about 3 minutes. Stir in the green curry paste and cook until fragrant, about 20 seconds. Work fast, so the paste doesn't burn. Immediately pour in the coconut milk and fish sauce, then increase the heat to high to bring to a boil.

When you see the boiling bubbles, add the sliced chicken breasts and cauliflower florets. Reduce the heat back to medium and simmer for 5 to 7 minutes. Add the bell pepper and cook for 2 to 3 minutes, until the chicken is fully cooked through and the veggies are tender but not too soft. Turn the heat off and stir in lime juice, then top with cilantro. Serve hot.

Grilled Chicken Breasts with Tahini Satay Sauce

Tahini is definitely a growing obsession of mine. It's delicious in both sweet and savory dishes, and that's exactly what you'll be experiencing with my tasty low-carb spin on satay. I've replaced traditional peanut butter with tahini because it adds a delicious complement to the dish. This grilled chicken is healthy and super quick to make.

Serves 4

Grilled Chicken Breasts

2 tsp (10 ml) coconut aminos

½ tsp chili powder

½ tsp garlic powder

½ tsp kosher salt

4 boneless, skinless chicken breasts, halved (2 lb [907 g] total)

Coconut oil cooking spray

¼ cup (4 g) chopped fresh cilantro leaves, for serving (optional)

Satay Sauce

¼ cup (60 g) tahini

1½ tbsp (23 ml) white wine vinegar

1 tbsp (15 ml) water

1 tbsp (15 ml) avocado oil

2 tsp (10 ml) hot sauce

1 tsp minced peeled fresh ginger

1 clove garlic, minced

To make the chicken: Combine the coconut aminos, chili powder, garlic powder and salt in a bowl. Rub the spice mixture evenly on the chicken breast halves. Heat a grill pan over medium-high heat and spray with cooking spray. Add the chicken to the pan and grill 6 to 8 minutes per side, or until cooked. Set aside when ready and let the chicken rest.

To make the satay sauce: Combine the tahini, vinegar, water, oil, hot sauce, ginger and garlic in a bowl. Whisk until smooth or blend with an immersion blender if you have one.

Spoon the tahini satay sauce over the chicken breasts and garnish with cilantro, if using.

30-Minute Butter Chicken

This low-carb dish is a winning favorite on my blog and among my readers. I decided to make it even more delightful by adding a silky touch of extra ghee and coconut milk, which gives the sauce a rich and creamy texture. The garam masala and spices combine to make this dish out-of-this-world delicious.

Serves 5

2 tbsp (30 g) clarified butter (ghee)

1 small red onion, diced

1–2 tbsp (7–14 g) coconut flour

1 tbsp (7 g) garam masala

1 tsp ground ginger

1 tsp curry powder

1½ tsp (9 g) kosher salt

½ tsp chili powder

1 tsp ground black pepper

1 (6-oz [170-g]) can low-sodium tomato paste

1 (13-oz [384-ml]) can full-fat organic coconut milk, plus more if needed

3 large boneless, skinless chicken breasts, cut into small cubes (1¾ lb [794 g] total)

Chopped fresh cilantro, for serving (optional)

4 cups (453 g) cooked cauliflower rice, for serving (optional)

Place a Dutch oven or a large saucepan over medium heat and add the ghee. Once heated, sauté the onion until fragrant, about 4 minutes. Add the coconut flour, garam masala, ginger, curry powder, salt, chili powder and pepper. Stir until the spices are well combined. Gradually stir in the tomato paste and coconut milk and let it simmer for about 5 minutes. Your sauce should have thickened by this point.

Gradually stir in the chicken until it is evenly coated in the sauce. Simmer for 7 to 9 minutes until the chicken is fully cooked. Reduce the heat to medium-low and let the butter chicken simmer for 10 minutes. If you find the sauce too thick, you can add more coconut milk or any unsweetened nut milk. Garnish with the cilantro and serve immediately with cauliflower rice (if using).

Chive Mandarin Chicken with Cauliflower Rice

When I was younger, I always looked forward to Sunday afternoons because my dad would take me out for Chinese food as one of our bonding traditions. Mandarin chicken was one of his favorite things to order. As a tribute to treasure my fondest memories with dear old dad, here's a quick and simple spin on the restaurant version you love. My low-carb mandarin chicken is healthier and tastes amazing. I use chives to add a delicate onion flavor that complements the orange chicken perfectly.

Serves 3

Orange Sauce

3 cloves garlic, minced

Juice of 1 ripe orange (½ cup [120 ml])

1 tsp orange zest

¼ cup (60 ml) coconut aminos

¼ cup (60 ml) freshly squeezed lemon juice

1½ tbsp (12 g) cornstarch

½ tsp ground ginger

Kosher salt and ground black pepper

Cauliflower Rice

1 tbsp (14 g) organic coconut oil

4 cups (340 g) store-bought riced cauliflower

Kosher salt and ground black pepper

Mandarin Chicken

2 boneless, skinless chicken breasts, cut into cubes (1¼ lb [567 g] total)

Kosher salt and ground black pepper

2 tbsp (30 ml) extra virgin olive oil

½ cup (24 g) chopped fresh chives, for serving

Red pepper flakes, for serving

To make the orange sauce: In a medium bowl, whisk together the garlic, orange juice, orange zest, coconut aminos, lemon juice, cornstarch, ginger, salt and pepper. Set aside.

To make the cauliflower rice: Heat the oil in a 12-inch (30-cm) skillet over medium-high heat. Add the cauliflower rice, and season with salt and pepper. Cook the cauliflower rice for about 2 to 3 minutes, then transfer to a serving bowl and keep warm. Wipe the skillet and set it aside for the mandarin chicken.

To make the chicken: Season the chicken with salt and pepper. Place the wiped skillet over medium-high heat and add the oil. Add the chicken and sauté for about 4 to 6 minutes, stirring occasionally until the chicken is browned and nearly cooked through. Pour in the orange sauce and stir to combine. You will notice it may thicken up a little, which is the goal. Bring the sauce to a boil for about 1 minute, then turn the heat off.

Serve the chicken with cauliflower rice topped with chives and red pepper flakes.

Chicken Ratatouille

If you've seen the movie *Ratatouille*, you know that Remy was determined to be the greatest chef in Paris. With my low-carb chicken ratatouille, the aim is simplicity, speed and great flavor—and I can promise you success in nailing all these areas happily. The flavor of this chicken ratatouille is that of a mild margherita with herbed chicken, which creates a marriage between Italian and French cuisine.

Serves 4

Ratatouille

2 tbsp (30 ml) extra virgin olive oil

1 small red onion, sliced

1 medium eggplant, sliced

2 zucchinis, sliced

2 cloves garlic, minced

1 medium yellow bell pepper, sliced

1 medium tomato, sliced

¼ cup (10 g) chopped fresh basil

¼ tsp kosher salt

Ground black pepper

Chicken

¼ cup (26 g) almond flour

4 boneless, skinless chicken breasts
(2 lb [907 g] total)

½ tsp kosher salt

½ tsp ground black pepper

1½ tbsp (8 g) dried oregano

2 tbsp (30 ml) extra virgin olive oil

To make the ratatouille: Heat the oil in a 12-inch (30-cm) skillet over medium-high heat. Sauté the onion and eggplant for 5 minutes, until fragrant and light brown around the edges. Add the zucchinis, garlic and bell pepper and sauté for about 8 minutes, until tender. Add the tomato, basil, salt and a sprinkle of pepper. Keep stirring until the mixture is cooked, about 3 to 5 minutes. Remove the veggies from the skillet and transfer to a serving dish. Keep warm. Wipe down your skillet.

To make the chicken: Place the almond flour on a plate for dredging. Season the chicken breasts with salt, pepper and oregano, then dredge the chicken in almond flour, shaking off the excess. Heat the oil over medium-high heat and place the chicken breasts in the skillet. Sear the chicken for 4 to 5 minutes on each side, until golden brown.

Remove the chicken from the skillet. Slice and serve with the ratatouille.

Cauliflower Turkey Chili

You can never go wrong with a big bowl of chili, especially when it's low carb, quick to make and delicious. My cauliflower turkey chili will be your new favorite go-to comfort food.

Serves 4

3 tbsp (45 ml) extra virgin olive oil

2–3 shallots, chopped

3 cloves garlic, minced

1½ tsp (9 g) kosher salt

2 tsp (5 g) chili powder

1 tsp Italian seasoning

1 lb (454 g) ground turkey

1½ cups (360 ml) brewed instant dark roast coffee

1 (14-oz [397-g]) can diced tomatoes with their juice

3 cups (400 g) frozen cauliflower florets

Chopped fresh cilantro, for serving

Heat the oil in a Dutch oven over medium-high heat. Working with a wooden spoon, sauté the shallots, garlic, salt, chili powder and Italian seasoning until fragrant, about 2 to 3 minutes. Add the ground turkey and break it up until you no longer see pink, about 3 minutes or so.

Add the instant coffee and simmer, covered, for about 8 minutes. Add the tomatoes and cauliflower, mixing up the tomatoes in the chili. Let it simmer, covered, for about 10 minutes, stirring occasionally. Garnish with cilantro and serve.

Chef's Note: Purchase prepared fresh or frozen cauliflower to use in your low-carb cooking so you'll always have it on hand and prepped. You do not have to thaw frozen cauliflower prior to use for most recipes. You can also use riced cauliflower for this recipe.

Sesame-Ginger Chicken Lettuce Wraps

This is like a healthy cross between a taco and a burrito, but better and even more flavorful. With the nuttiness of the sesame seeds and warm, sweet hints of ginger, this low-carb lettuce wrap exceeds all expectations.

Serves 5

1 tbsp (9 g) minced garlic

1 tbsp (6 g) minced fresh ginger

¼ cup (60 ml) sesame oil

¼ cup (60 ml) coconut aminos

4 tsp (12 g) sesame seeds

1 tsp kosher salt

1 tsp ground black pepper

1 tsp red pepper flakes

1 lb (454 g) ground chicken

12 green leaf lettuce leaves, for serving

Chopped chives, for serving

To make the sesame-ginger sauce: In a small bowl, whisk together the garlic, ginger, sesame oil, coconut aminos, sesame seeds, salt, pepper and red pepper flakes. Set aside.

In a 12-inch (30-cm) skillet, cook and crumble the ground chicken over medium-high heat until you no longer see pink, about 2 to 3 minutes. Stir in the sesame-ginger sauce and cook for 5 minutes, until fully cooked and fragrant. Remove from the heat.

Serve the chicken on lettuce wraps, straining some of the liquid. Top with chives.

Parmesan-Sumac Chicken and Crispy Kale

If you have never tried sumac, then you've been missing out. Sumac is a Middle Eastern spice that is similar to lemon but slightly stronger with more botanical notes. It pairs beautifully with poultry dishes like this delicious low-carb sumac chicken, with all the goodness of crispy Lacinato kale and cheesy Parmesan.

Serves 4

1 (6-oz [170-g]) bunch Lacinato kale, stemmed and torn into large pieces

2 tbsp (30 ml) extra virgin olive oil, divided

4 boneless, skinless chicken breasts (2 lb [907 g] total)

½ tbsp (4 g) sumac

4 sprigs of fresh thyme, divided

¼ tsp kosher salt

½ tsp black pepper

2 oz (57 g) Parmigiano-Reggiano cheese, freshly grated

¼ tsp red pepper flakes

Preheat your oven to broil. Place a rimmed baking sheet on the wire rack at the top of the oven.

In a separate bowl, massage the kale leaves with 1 tablespoon (15 ml) of oil. Sprinkle the chicken with sumac, thyme sprigs, salt and pepper, then carefully remove the pan from the oven wearing ovenproof mitts. Add 1 tablespoon (15 ml) of oil to the sheet pan and tilt the pan to coat, then add the chicken to the pan and return it to the oven. Broil the chicken for 15 to 17 minutes.

Remove the chicken from the oven and place it on a cutting board, then immediately add the kale mixture to the hot pan. Return the pan to the oven and broil until the kale is crisp, 3 to 5 minutes. Remove the pan from the oven.

Return the chicken to the pan and top the chicken with cheese and red pepper flakes. Serve hot.

Salsa Verde Chicken Thighs

This is definitely a barbecue showstopper, a date night surprise or a weeknight delight. Unlike the bolder, garlic flavor of a chimichurri or gremolata, salsa verde delivers the lighter, tangy and sweeter flavors of lime, mint and cilantro, with a slight kick of white wine vinegar. Oh yes, you will be winning weeknight dinners and all festivities with salsa verde on the menu.

Serves 4

Salsa Verde

1 cup (16 g) fresh cilantro leaves

½ cup (46 g) fresh mint leaves

1 tbsp (9 g) capers

Juice of 1 lime

1 tsp white wine vinegar

1½ tbsp (23 ml) honey Dijon mustard

2–3 mini pickles, or 1 regular-sized pickle

5–8 tbsp (75–120 ml) extra virgin olive oil

Baked Chicken Thighs

2 tbsp (30 ml) extra virgin olive oil

6 boneless, skinless chicken thighs, fat trimmed (2 lb [907 g] total)

Roasted bell peppers, for serving (optional)

Preheat your oven to 425°F (220°C, or gas mark 7).

To make the salsa verde: Combine the cilantro, mint, capers, lime juice, vinegar, Dijon mustard, pickles and oil in a food processor. Puree until smooth, then set aside.

To make the chicken thighs: Grease a rimmed baking sheet with the oil, tilting to spread. In a large bowl, add the chicken thighs, then scoop about ½ cup (120 ml) of the salsa verde into the bowl. Toss the chicken, rubbing it around generously. You may have some sauce left over in the bowl depending on the size of your chicken thighs.

Place the coated chicken on the rimmed baking sheet and transfer it to the oven. Bake for 25 minutes. This dish pairs well with roasted bell peppers.

If serving with roasted bell peppers, line a baking sheet with foil. Cut the peppers in half and remove the seeds. Place in the oven on the bottom rack and let them cook while the chicken bakes. Cook for 25 minutes.

Chef's Note: The leftover salsa verde stays fresh in the fridge for up to 2 days.

French Chili Chicken with Lemon Butter Sauce

This is where having a good stash of alcohol reigns supreme. This flavorful delicacy uses zesty lemon and butter with the addition of dry sherry in the sauce to enhance the flavor and add a unique touch. Although this low-carb dish doesn't have French origins as the name implies, using Pernod instead of sherry might add a slightly sweet anise flavor for a French twist.

Serves 4

4 eggs

2 tbsp (30 ml) almond milk

1 cup (112 g) coconut flour

1 tbsp (18 g) kosher salt, plus more for seasoning

1 tsp ground black pepper, plus more for seasoning

Pinch of cayenne pepper

4 boneless, skinless chicken breast cutlets, pounded flat (¾ lb [340 g] total)

2 tbsp (30 ml) extra virgin olive oil

1 tbsp (14 g) unsalted grass-fed butter

1 cup (240 ml) low-sodium vegetable broth

½ cup (120 ml) dry sherry or Pernod

Juice of ½ lemon

¼ cup (57 g) cold unsalted grass-fed butter, cut into chunks

1–2 small red Thai chili peppers, chopped

1 tbsp (4 g) chopped fresh flat-leaf parsley

Pan-toasted asparagus, for serving (optional)

In a shallow bowl, beat the eggs and milk together. In another shallow bowl, whisk the coconut flour, salt, pepper and cayenne together.

Gently press your chicken into the flour mixture to coat, shaking off the excess flour. Dip it into the egg mixture and coat completely. Heat the oil and butter together in a 12-inch (30-cm) skillet over medium heat. Cook the chicken in the heated oil until lightly browned, about 3 minutes per side. Transfer the chicken to a plate and set aside.

Add the broth, sherry and lemon juice to the same skillet. Stir as you bring it to a boil and cook until the sauce is reduced by half, about 1 to 2 minutes. Remove from the heat and add cold butter chunks and chili peppers, then stir until the butter is melted and the sauce is shiny and thickened, about 1 to 2 minutes. Stir the parsley into the sauce and season with salt and pepper. If you want a thicker sauce, simply mix 1 teaspoon of cornstarch with 1 tablespoon (15 ml) of water and stir into the sauce.

Return the chicken to the skillet over medium heat and spoon the sauce over the top. Cook until your chicken is heated through and no longer pink in the center, about 2 to 3 minutes more. This pairs well with pan-toasted asparagus, if using.

Chef's Note: For instructions on how to cook pan-toasted asparagus, see page 142.

Chicken Piccata

This lemony chicken piccata is as simple and delicious as the name implies. With the saltiness of the capers and fresh tang from the lemon, the seasonings are minimal but produce a quick and surprisingly tasty low-carb dish.

Serves 4

4 boneless, skinless chicken breasts, halved (2 lb [907 g] total)

½ tsp cayenne pepper

Kosher salt and ground black pepper

½ cup (42 g) coconut flour, for dredging

2 tbsp (30 ml) extra virgin olive oil

1 tbsp (9 g) capers, drained

½ cup (120 ml) chicken broth

2 tbsp (30 ml) freshly squeezed lemon juice

¼ cup (60 ml) water

3 tbsp (42 g) cold unsalted grass-fed butter, cut in ¼-inch (6-mm) slices

2 tbsp (8 g) chopped fresh Italian parsley

3 cups (340 g) cooked cauliflower rice, for serving (optional)

Place the chicken breasts between two layers of plastic wrap and pound flat to about ½ inch (1 cm) thick. This will ensure that the chicken comes out extra crispy. Season both sides of the chicken breasts with cayenne, salt and pepper. Dredge lightly in coconut flour and shake off any excess.

Heat the oil in a 12-inch (30-cm) skillet over medium-high heat, then place the chicken breasts in the pan and reduce the heat to medium. Cook the chicken for about 5 minutes per side until browned and cooked through. Transfer to a plate and set aside.

Add the capers to the skillet and sauté, smashing them lightly to release brine, about 30 seconds. Pour the broth into the skillet and cook for about 2 minutes. Scrape up any browned bits from the skillet.

Stir the lemon juice, water and butter into the broth mixture and stir continuously to form a sauce, about 2 minutes. Reduce the heat to low and stir the parsley through the sauce. Return the chicken breasts to the skillet and cook for 1 to 2 minutes, until heated through. Serve the chicken with sauce spooned over the top and with a side of cauliflower rice (if using).

Chef's Note: If you want the sauce a little thicker, simply mix 1 teaspoon of cornstarch with 1 to 2 tablespoons (15 to 30 ml) of water and pour into the sauce closer to the end of the cooking time.

Bold-Flavored Seafood

I have been a city girl for most of my adult life, and of course it is common for big cities to be home to a wide selection of restaurants. No matter where you are and what you are craving, you can find a restaurant on every street with a seafood menu. As much as I enjoy a delicious seafood platter every now and again, there are two factors in seafood dining that can be challenging. You either get a small selection of high-quality overpriced seafood, or you get pub-style fish and chips, which is more economical but not necessarily the healthiest option. Although there are restaurants that are diversifying their seafood menus, nothing can compete with the menu that you create in your very own kitchen.

This chapter covers all things seafood. I've created the most delicious low-carb versions of seafood dishes from some of my favorite restaurants, such as swapping the panko-crusted halibut for my Halibut en Papillote with Poached Cauliflower (page 91). Each recipe is guaranteed to give you an elegant and well-plated delight in under 30 minutes. You might as well bring the restaurant to your own home.

Wine Butter Trout with Asparagus and Tomato

This is arguably fine dining at its best, and it comes together in less than 30 minutes in your kitchen. My low-carb rendition blends all the flavors of butter and wine with a sprinkle of herbs, giving the trout a light and flaky texture and a gorgeous aroma. Using dry white wine in this dish enhances the flavor profile, while making your cooking experience more fun. Weeknight dinner never looked so good.

Serves 4

¼ cup (57 g) unsalted grass-fed butter, divided

2 lb (907 g) rainbow trout

2 tbsp (30 ml) white wine

½ tsp kosher salt

½ tsp ground black pepper

½ tsp garlic powder

1 tsp dried parsley

1 tsp dried thyme

¾ cup (112 g) cherry tomatoes on the vine

20 asparagus stalks, ends chopped

2 tbsp (30 ml) extra virgin olive oil

Preheat your oven to 400°F (200°C, or gas mark 6). Lightly butter a large rectangular 12-inch (30-cm) cast-iron skillet with about 2 tablespoons (28 g) of butter, or two separate round skillets with 1 tablespoon (14 g) of butter each. This will allow the skin of the trout to crisp when it goes in the oven. Add the trout to the skillet.

In a small bowl, melt the remaining butter, then combine the butter, wine, salt, pepper, garlic powder, parsley and thyme. Brush the mixture on the trout until all areas are coated.

Add the tomatoes and asparagus to the skillet. Brush the tomatoes and asparagus with oil: about 1 tablespoon (15 ml) for the asparagus and 1 tablespoon (15 ml) for the cherry tomatoes.

Transfer the skillet to the oven and bake for 15 minutes. Serve immediately.

Mouthwatering Mustard Crab Cakes

I've always remembered restaurant crab cakes as being worthwhile, mainly due to the party going on in my mouth because of how deliciously breaded, flavorful and moist they were. I want you to have a taste of that, but with a healthier twist that has fewer carbs and will take you less than 30 minutes to make. You deserve delicious experiences too.

Serves 4

2 lb (907 g) wild-caught crabmeat

2 eggs, whisked

2 tbsp (30 g) mayonnaise

2 tbsp (30 ml) Dijon mustard

2 shallots, minced

2 cloves garlic, minced

2 tbsp (6 g) Italian seasoning

2 tbsp (11 g) dried oregano

Fresh chopped chives, for serving

Cooked palmini, for serving (optional)

Preheat your oven to 350°F (175°C, or gas mark 4). Line a baking sheet with parchment paper and set it aside.

In a large mixing bowl, combine the crabmeat, eggs, mayonnaise, Dijon mustard, shallots, garlic, Italian seasoning and oregano. Form the crab mixture into 8 mini cakes, about the size of the palm of your hand. Place the crab cakes on the lined baking sheet and bake in the oven for 20 to 25 minutes, until cooked and lightly browned around the edges.

Top the crab cakes with chives. This pairs well with cooked palmini linguine, if using.

Chef's Note: For information on how to cook palmini, see page 120.

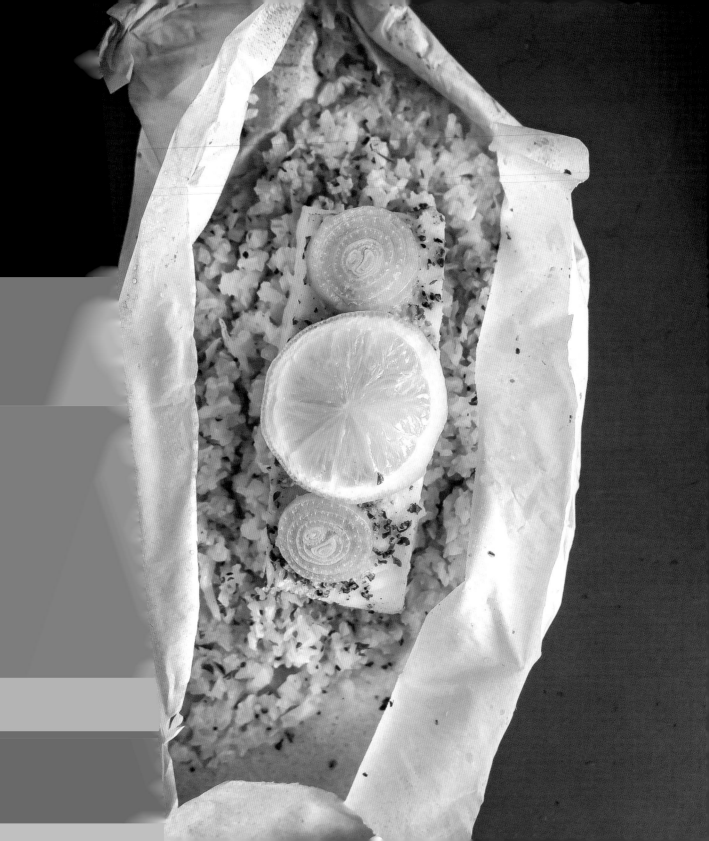

Halibut en Papillote with Poached Cauliflower

The first time I tried halibut en papillote was at an airport lounge during a layover when I was traveling through Europe one summer. "En papillote" means to cook in paper. The technique steams your fish and veggies all at once and very quickly as well, while retaining its flakiness and flavor. I'm dishing out a delicious version that is quick, low carb and nutritious.

Serves 4

Olive oil, for the parchment

2 cups (226 g) store-bought cauliflower rice, divided

Kosher salt and freshly cracked black pepper

1 tsp onion powder

4 tsp (16 g) unsalted grass-fed butter, melted and divided

4 (8-oz [226-g]) halibut fillets

1 tsp garlic powder

1½ tbsp (3 g) dried parsley, divided

2 shallots, thinly sliced

½ small lemon, thinly sliced

Preheat your oven to 400°F (200°C, or gas mark 6). Cut out four 15 x 15–inch (38 x 38–cm) sheets of parchment and fold them in half, then cut the pointy edges until you form a heart shape. Brush the heart-shaped pieces of parchment with oil, especially around the edges so that they seal better. Place them on 2 large baking sheets.

Top the right side of the heart of the prepared parchment papers with the cauliflower rice, then season with salt, pepper, onion powder and butter. Add the halibut and season it with salt, pepper, garlic powder and parsley. Top the halibut with shallots and lemon slices, then seal the edges of the paper by bringing the left side of the heart to the other side, covering the halibut until you get a half-moon. Seal the edges by rolling the parchment paper inward toward the halibut, creating a sealed pouch for the fish. Repeat the process for the remaining halibut.

Bake for 15 minutes. Cut the top of the parchment and serve hot. Note that the cauliflower will have a bit of bite to it, which is intended to complement the texture of fish.

Rosemary Aioli Baked Trout

It can't get more lazy-proof than this, but lazy-proof doesn't mean boring, and this low-carb rosemary aioli baked trout is far from that. You won't walk into a seafood restaurant without being served a side of aioli, so I spiced things up a bit by adding rosemary to give it a kick of woody earthiness that blends well with the creaminess of the sauce and the healthy fats from the trout. Paired with a side of fresh greens, your 30-minute weeknight dinner will be a sure winner.

Serves 4

1 cup (240 g) mayonnaise

2 cloves garlic, minced

1 tbsp (2 g) chopped fresh rosemary

Kosher salt and ground black pepper

2 lb (907 g) rainbow trout

1 lemon, sliced into wedges

Field green salad, for serving

Preheat your oven to 400°F (200°C, or gas mark 6). Line a baking sheet with parchment paper.

In a food processor, combine the mayonnaise, garlic, rosemary and salt and pepper to taste. Puree until smooth, then set aside.

Place your trout on the baking sheet, then spread about 2 to 3 tablespoons (30 to 45 ml) of the aioli on the trout until coated. Sprinkle with salt and pepper. Bake in the oven for 15 minutes, then turn your oven to broil for 2 to 3 minutes. Top with lemon and serve on a bed of fresh greens.

Citrus-Herbed Salmon with Garlic Butter Sauce

This low-carb, garlicky, zesty and buttery salmon is so flavorful and extremely yummy. It gives you all the feel-good vibes in every bite without the guilt in your belly or your wallet, especially since seafood dining can be a pocket pincher. Plus, it only takes 30 minutes to make, so all the more to love.

Serves 4

4 (18-oz [510-g]) salmon fillets

1 tsp kosher salt

½ tsp ground black pepper

2 tsp (1 g) dried thyme

3 tbsp (45 ml) lime juice, divided

1 tbsp (15 ml) extra virgin olive oil

3 tbsp (42 g) unsalted grass-fed butter

6 cloves garlic, minced

¼ cup (15 g) chopped fresh Italian parsley leaves, divided

4 lime slices, for serving

3 cups (340 g) cooked cauliflower rice, for serving (optional)

Rub the salmon fillets with salt, pepper and thyme. Rub about 2 teaspoons (10 ml) of lime juice on the salmon fillets to get in all the flavor, then set aside.

Heat the oil in a 12-inch (30-cm) skillet over medium-high heat. Place the salmon fillets in the skillet flesh side down and sear undisturbed for 4 to 5 minutes, until lightly browned. Flip the fillets and sear skin side down for 2 minutes.

Add the butter, garlic, 2 tablespoons (8 g) of parsley and the remaining lime juice. Baste your salmon and continue cooking for 2 minutes until the butter is slightly browned. Garnish with the remaining parsley. Serve immediately with the lime slices and the cauliflower rice (if using).

Chili-Lime Salmon and Asparagus

The first time I came across chili-lime salmon was at a pub where I was watching a soccer game. The flavors of the salmon blew my mind, and it was served with crispy mashed potatoes. As delicious as it was, I knew it wasn't sustainable, but this low-carb chili-lime salmon with crispy asparagus definitely is. You get the smokiness from the chili and a fresh tang from the lime—it doesn't get any better than that.

Serves 4

⅓ cup (80 ml) coconut aminos

3 tbsp (45 ml) fresh lime juice

1 tbsp (15 ml) avocado oil, plus more for greasing

20 asparagus stalks, ends chopped

1 tsp kosher salt, plus more for seasoning

½ tsp ground black pepper, plus more for seasoning

4 (18-oz [510-g]) salmon fillets

½ tsp chili powder

¼ cup (15 g) chopped fresh parsley

4 lime slices

Preheat your oven to 400°F (200°C, or gas mark 6). Line a baking sheet with foil, slightly tented around the edges.

In a medium bowl, whisk together the coconut aminos and lime juice, then set aside. Grease the foil with some oil, then top with asparagus, and drizzle 1 tablespoon (15 ml) of oil on the asparagus. Season with salt and pepper. Bake for 10 minutes, then remove from the oven.

Move the asparagus to the edges of the pan and place the salmon in the middle, then rub the salmon with 1 teaspoon salt, ½ teaspoon pepper and chili powder. Top with the lime juice mixture and the parsley.

Slide 1 lime slice underneath each salmon fillet and cover the top of the baking sheet with another sheet of foil. Return to the oven and bake for 13 to 15 minutes.

Creamy Basil-Coconut Scallops with Zucchini

Scallops are a luxury that we all deserve to enjoy every now and again. This recipe is quick and easy to cook, and it only requires basic spices to enhance the natural flavor profiles. This creamy low-carb delight is rich, herby and provides just the right amount of comfort for those fall or winter blues.

Serves 4

1 lb (454 g) dry scallops

½ tsp kosher salt

¼ tsp ground black pepper

2 tbsp (30 ml) extra virgin olive oil

2 tbsp (28 g) unsalted grass-fed butter

2 cloves garlic, minced

1 tbsp (15 g) basil paste

½ tsp dried thyme

¼ cup (60 ml) vegetable broth

1 cup (240 ml) full-fat coconut milk

4 zucchinis, spiralized

Pat the scallops dry with a paper towel and squeeze out any excess moisture, even if you purchase dry scallops. Season the scallops with salt and pepper.

Place a skillet over medium-high heat and add the oil. Once the oil becomes hot, add the scallops, making sure they are not touching each other. Sear one side for 3 minutes undisturbed. Flip the scallops and let the scallops sear for 2 to 3 minutes. Remove the scallops from the pan and transfer them to a plate, then scrape up the browned bits and discard.

In the same pan, add the butter, garlic, basil paste and thyme. Cook until fragrant, about 1 minute. Add the broth and coconut milk. Bring to a simmer, about 2 minutes, then add a dash of salt and pepper. While simmering, add the zucchini and cook for about 2 minutes, then turn the heat off. Return the scallops to the sauce and serve.

Cajun Orange Sesame Shrimp Shirataki

Orange sesame shrimp is a favorite you'll find at a lot of all-you-can-eat Chinese restaurants. Throw in a dash of Cajun spice and you officially give it your unique flare, while keeping it low carb, quick and delicious. With the addition of shirataki, which has zero net carbs, you can enjoy noodles for dinner without any guilt. Oh yes, it's orange, spice and everything nice.

Serves 4

Orange Sauce

Juice of 1 orange

1 clove garlic, minced

1 tsp minced fresh ginger

½ tsp Cajun spice

1 tbsp (15 ml) coconut aminos

½ tsp hot sauce

2 tbsp (30 ml) hot water

Shrimp Shirataki

4 cups (1 kg) raw shrimp, peeled and deveined

1 tsp Cajun spice

2 (8-oz [226-g]) packages shirataki noodles

2 tbsp (30 ml) extra virgin olive oil

1 red bell pepper, sliced

1 tsp sesame seeds, for serving

Chopped scallions, for serving

To make the orange sauce: In a small bowl, combine the orange juice, garlic, ginger, Cajun spice, coconut aminos, hot sauce and hot water. Whisk the sauce together, and set it aside.

To make the shrimp shirataki, rub the shrimp with the Cajun spice. Pour the sauce over the shrimp and let it sit for about 10 minutes.

Prepare the shirataki by draining the brine and rinsing it under warm water. Cook the shirataki according to package instructions.

Heat the oil in a skillet over medium heat, then add the shrimp and bell pepper with orange sauce. Cover the skillet and let the sauce simmer for 2 to 3 minutes. When ready, add the shirataki to the sauce, stirring until the shirataki is coated in the sauce. The sauce is going to be thin, so that the shirataki can soak it up; shirataki can be rather bland on its own.

Transfer the shrimp shirataki to a serving plate and top with sesame seeds and scallions. Serve immediately.

Pan-Seared Cod with Cilantro, Lime and Garlic

Every time I've had cod at a restaurant, it has always been served breaded and deep-fried with a side of tartar. My pan-seared cod is a healthier spin with a low-carb twist. It packs in all the wonderful fresh flavors from herbs and citrus, while also cutting down your cooking time to 30 minutes.

Serves 4

Cilantro, Lime and Garlic Topping

2 cups (32 g) finely chopped fresh cilantro leaves

1 lime, zested and juiced

1 clove garlic, minced

¼ tsp kosher salt

¼ tsp ground black pepper

¼ cup (60 ml) extra virgin olive oil

Pan-Seared Cod

2 tbsp (30 ml) extra virgin olive oil

4 (6-oz [170-g]) wild Alaskan cod fillets

Kosher salt and ground black pepper

2 tbsp (28 g) unsalted grass-fed butter

Salad, cauliflower rice or fresh greens, for serving

To make the cilantro, lime and garlic: In a food processor, combine the cilantro, lime, garlic, salt, pepper and oil. Puree until smooth, then set aside.

To make the cod, heat the oil in a 12-inch (30-cm) skillet over medium-high heat. Sprinkle the cod with salt and pepper, about ⅛ teaspoon for each fillet. Once the pan is hot, sear the cod for 3 to 4 minutes on the first side. Add the butter to the pan and allow it to melt. Once the butter has melted, flip the cod and finish cooking it on the other side, 3 to 4 minutes more, or until just cooked through.

Transfer the cod fillets to a serving plate and top with 1 to 2 tablespoons (15 to 30 ml) of the cilantro mixture. Serve with a side salad, cauliflower rice or a bed of fresh greens.

Sesame-Balsamic Tuna Steaks with Kale Sauté

Tuna steaks are probably the easiest low-carb meal you could ever make, mainly because of the searing technique involved in cooking them. They can be the most expensive to eat at a restaurant, but can be much less expensive if you cook them in your kitchen. Except for oils and spices, you only need five ingredients to make this dish a quick and easy culinary success.

Serves 2

2 (3.5-oz [99-g]) fresh or frozen tuna steaks

¼ cup (60 ml) sugar-free balsamic reduction, store-bought or homemade

2 tbsp (18 g) sesame seeds

2 tbsp (30 ml) avocado oil

1 tbsp (15 ml) extra virgin olive oil

2 cups (134 g) baby kale

½ cup (50 g) Tomberry® tomatoes

Kosher salt and ground black pepper

Coat the tuna steaks in the balsamic reduction, then sprinkle both sides with sesame seeds. Heat the avocado oil in a 12-inch (30-cm) cast-iron skillet over high heat, then sear the tuna steaks for exactly 45 seconds. Flip the tuna and sear the reverse for 45 seconds, until the seeds have toasted. Transfer to a chopping board and let the tuna steaks rest for 2 to 3 minutes. The steaks are supposed to be served medium-rare.

Reduce the heat to medium-high and switch skillets. Heat the olive oil, then add the kale and tomatoes to the pan. Season with salt and pepper. Sauté until the kale is withered, about 2 to 3 minutes, then remove the pan from the heat and transfer the kale sauté to a plate. Slice the tuna steaks and serve on top of the kale sauté.

Chef's Note: You can make your own balsamic reduction at home days in advance if you'd prefer. All you have to do is heat 1 cup (240 ml) of balsamic vinegar over medium-high heat in a small saucepan and stir occasionally until reduced, about 10 minutes. Store in an airtight container and use as a glaze for salads and meats.

Garlic Butter Scallops with Broccolini

Some people may be too intimidated to cook scallops, especially since they can be quite pricey. But I'm bringing the gourmet to your home with banging flavors from garlic, parsley and sizzling butter, all in a low-carb package and accomplished in 30 minutes.

Serves 3

Broccolini

1 tbsp (18 g) kosher salt

½ lb (226 g) broccolini, stems chopped

2 tbsp (30 ml) extra virgin olive oil

3 cloves garlic, minced

Scallops

1 lb (454 g) dry scallops

½ tsp kosher salt

¼ tsp ground black pepper

2 tbsp (30 ml) olive oil

3 tbsp (42 g) grass-fed butter

4 cloves garlic, minced

¼ cup (60 ml) bone broth or low-sodium vegetable broth

⅓ cup (20 g) chopped fresh parsley, for serving

To make the broccolini: In a saucepan, bring 4 cups (960 ml) of water with the salt to a boil over high heat. Add the broccolini. Boil for 2 minutes until tender but crisp. When ready, immediately immerse the broccolini in a bowl of ice water, and let it sit for 2 to 3 minutes. In the meantime, place a skillet over medium-high heat and add the oil. Once hot, sauté the garlic for about 30 seconds, until fragrant. Add the broccolini and stir until coated in garlic for 1 minute. Remove from the heat and keep warm.

To make the scallops: Pat them dry with a paper towel and press out any excess moisture, even if you purchase dry scallops. Season the scallops with salt and pepper. Heat the oil in a 12-inch (30-cm) skillet over medium-high heat until hot. Add the scallops, making sure they aren't crowded or sticking together in the pan. Fry for 3 minutes undisturbed, then flip and fry the reverse side for 3 minutes. Remove the scallops from the pan and transfer to a plate, leaving the pan on the stove to make your garlic butter sauce.

Melt the butter in the same pan, scraping up the browned bits. Add the garlic and cook for 30 seconds. Pour in the broth and let it simmer until the sauce reduces, 2 to 3 minutes. Turn the heat off and return the scallops to the pan to coat in the sauce. Top with parsley and serve with the broccolini.

Blackened Salmon with Pistachio Pesto and Salad

Blackened salmon mimics the smoky-earthy char you enjoy from cedar plank salmon, and you can achieve this easy low-carb version in less than 30 minutes. Combined with pistachio pesto to give it a subtle sweetness with a nice kick of fresh herbs, you may think twice before sharing your dinner with anyone else.

Serves 4

Pistachio Pesto

¾ cup (23 g) arugula

½ cup (30 g) chopped fresh parsley

⅓ cup (41 g) raw pistachios, shelled and unsalted

2 tbsp (30 ml) lemon juice

1 clove garlic, minced

½ cup (120 ml) extra virgin olive oil

¼ cup (25 g) freshly grated Parmesan cheese

¼ tsp kosher salt

¼ tsp ground black pepper

Blackened Salmon

4 (4-oz [113-g]) salmon fillets, skin-on

½ tsp smoked paprika

½ tsp garlic powder

½ tsp kosher salt

½ tsp ground black pepper

2 tbsp (30 ml) extra virgin olive oil

Field green salad, for serving

Lemon wedges, for serving (optional)

To make the pistachio pesto: In a food processor, pulse the arugula, parsley, pistachios, lemon juice, garlic, oil, Parmesan, salt and pepper until smooth. Scoop out about ½ cup (120 ml) and reserve it for the salmon. The rest of the pesto can be stored in the fridge for 5 days.

Lay out the salmon on a chopping board. In a small bowl, combine the paprika, garlic powder, salt and pepper. Rub each fillet individually. Heat the oil in a 12-inch (30-cm) skillet over medium-high heat. Once the oil is hot, place the salmon flesh side down in the hot oil and sear for 3 to 4 minutes. Flip the salmon skin side down and sear for 4 to 6 minutes until crispy.

Transfer the salmon to a serving plate and top with pistachio pesto. Serve with a salad and lemon wedges, if using.

Cilantro-Lime Shrimp and "Grits"

My aunt owns a small café in Atlanta, and she makes the best grits enriched with all the goodness of texture, heat and, of course, carbs. I wanted to draw inspiration from that and create a version that combines everything I know and love about her grits, while keeping it low carb, simple and easy to make by using cauliflower instead of cornmeal. This cilantro-lime shrimp is still creamy, zesty, spicy and all things wonderful, without the worry of carbs or the long cooking time.

Serves 4

3 tbsp (42 g) unsalted grass-fed butter, divided

3½ cups (396 g) store-bought cauliflower rice

1 cup (240 ml) heavy cream

½ tsp kosher salt, plus more for seasoning

½ tsp ground black pepper, plus more for seasoning

⅓ cup (33 g) grated Parmesan cheese

1¼ lb (567 g) peeled and deveined shrimp

¼ tsp paprika

2 large cloves garlic, minced

¼ cup (4 g) roughly chopped fresh cilantro

Juice of 1 lime

Heat 1 tablespoon (14 g) of butter in a medium-sized saucepan over medium-high heat. Add the cauliflower rice, heavy cream and ½ teaspoon each of salt and pepper. Bring to a simmer, stirring frequently, until smooth like a porridge. Cook for 10 minutes, then stir in the Parmesan cheese. Set aside and keep warm.

Season the shrimp with salt, pepper and paprika. Heat the remaining butter in another skillet over medium-high heat. Add the garlic to the pan and sauté for 45 seconds until fragrant. Add the shrimp and cook for 4 minutes, tossing until no longer pink. Turn the heat off, and stir in the cilantro and lime juice. Serve with the grits.

Grilled Swordfish with Cannellini-Herb Butter

Grilled swordfish topped with herbed butter is a combo that is so simple and yet so perfect. Packed in a buttery ensemble of chives, dill and parsley, it adds a fresh and flavorful kick to the swordfish that makes it oh so delicious.

Serves 4

Cannellini-Herb Butter

1 cup (177 g) canned cannellini beans, drained

1 tbsp (15 ml) bean brine (aquafaba)

½ cup (114 g) unsalted grass-fed butter, softened

¼ tsp kosher salt

¼ tsp ground black pepper

2 tbsp (6 g) chopped fresh chives

2 tbsp (8 g) chopped fresh parsley

1 tbsp (4 g) chopped fresh dill (optional)

1 shallot, chopped

Grilled Swordfish

4 (6-oz [170-g]) swordfish steaks, about 1 inch (2.5 cm) thick

Extra virgin olive oil

Kosher salt and ground black pepper

Arugula salad, for serving

To make the cannellini-herb butter: In a food processor, combine the beans, bean brine, butter, salt, pepper, chives, parsley, dill (if using) and shallot. Puree until smooth and creamy. Scoop the cannellini-herb butter into a jar and set aside, keeping it at room temperature.

To make the swordfish: Rub the swordfish with a drizzle of oil on both sides. Season with a sprinkle of salt and pepper on both sides. Heat a grill pan over medium-high heat, then add the swordfish and grill about 4 minutes per side, until golden brown.

Top the swordfish with 2 tablespoons (28 g) of the butter, serve with the arugula salad and extra herb butter on the side and enjoy.

Seared Snapper with Summer Basil Salsa

This dish represents everything you love about patio dining—the colors alone are enough to make you want to throw a summer dinner party. It's low carb and comes together in 30 minutes, and it's full of fresh bold basil, blackberries, juicy tomato salsa and crispy seared snapper.

Serves 4

Seared Snapper

4 (6-oz [170-g]) skin-on red snapper fillets

1 tsp kosher salt

½ tsp ground black pepper

1 tbsp (15 ml) grapeseed oil

Basil Salsa

1 cup (145 g) chopped blackberries or strawberries

2 cups (300 g) cherry tomatoes, halved

¼ cup (10 g) chopped fresh basil

3 tbsp (45 ml) extra virgin olive oil

1 tbsp (15 ml) white wine vinegar

Baked eggplant, for serving (optional)

To make the snapper, flip the snapper skin side up and make 2 sharp lines using a knife. This will allow the fish to absorb the flavors of the spices when searing in the pan. Season the fish generously with salt and pepper. Heat the grapeseed oil in a 12-inch (30-cm) skillet over medium-high heat. Add the snapper, skin side down, and cook for 8 minutes until golden brown and crispy. Flip and cook the reverse side for 3 to 4 minutes. Remove from the pan and keep warm.

To make the salsa: In a medium bowl, combine the blackberries, tomatoes, basil, oil and vinegar. Toss until well combined.

Serve the red snapper with the salsa. This pairs well with baked eggplant, if using.

Chef's Note: Cooking the eggplant will make the total cooking time a little over 30 minutes, but here is the perfect baked eggplant recipe if you want an additional side. Preheat the oven to 400°F (200°C, or gas mark 6). Line a baking sheet with parchment paper.

Slice the eggplant in half lengthwise, then cut each half into quarters lengthwise. Place the eggplant onto the baking sheet with the skin side down. Brush each piece with olive oil (3 tablespoons [45 ml] total) and season generously with salt and pepper.

Roast in the preheated oven until softened and golden brown, 25 to 30 minutes. Remove from the oven and sprinkle with lemon juice. Serve hot.

Tuna Cakes with Gremolata

These quick and flavorful tuna cakes give a new elegance to canned tuna, with the lovely flavors of Dijon, chives and hot sauce along with a zesty pairing of gremolata. Choose canned tuna infused with olive oil instead of spring water for better texture and flavor.

Serves 4

Gremolata

1 cup (60 g) packed fresh Italian parsley

1–2 cloves garlic

Zest of 1 small lemon

2 tsp (10 ml) lemon juice

½ cup (120 ml) extra virgin olive oil

⅛–¼ tsp kosher salt

⅛–¼ tsp ground black pepper

Pinch of red pepper flakes

Tuna Cakes

4 (6-oz [170-g]) cans olive oil tuna

4 tsp (20 ml) Dijon mustard

2 tbsp (30 ml) Meyer lemon juice

2 tbsp (30 ml) water

¼ cup (15 g) chopped fresh parsley

¼ cup (12 g) chopped fresh chives

Dash of kosher salt and ground black pepper

½ tsp hot sauce

2 eggs

¼ cup (60 ml) extra virgin olive oil

Steamed broccoli, for serving (optional)

To make the gremolata: In a food processor, combine the parsley, garlic, lemon zest, lemon juice, oil, salt, pepper and red pepper flakes. Puree until smooth. Set aside.

To make the tuna: Drain the tuna. In a large bowl, combine the tuna with the Dijon mustard, lemon juice, water, parsley, chives, salt, pepper, hot sauce and eggs.

Divide into 8 portions and form cakes. Heat the oil in a skillet over medium-high heat and fry the cakes, at least 4 minutes per side. When ready, serve with a side of gremolata and steamed broccoli (if using).

Mexican Baked Cod

I never knew a dish so divine existed until I tried baked cod at one of my favorite Mexican restaurants in my city. The star of this dish is salsa, adding a saucy and spicy kick. Although traditional versions are topped with tortilla chips, this low-carb version is finished with sharp Cheddar and a dash of cilantro.

Serves 4

1½ lb (680 g) wild-caught cod

1 cup (260 g) organic store-bought salsa

1 cup (113 g) shredded sharp Cheddar cheese, or aged Cheddar

1 avocado, peeled, pitted and sliced

¼ cup (60 ml) crème fraîche or sour cream

¼ cup (4 g) chopped fresh cilantro or parsley

Pan-toasted asparagus, for serving (optional)

Preheat your oven to 400°F (200°C, or gas mark 6). Lightly grease an 8 x 12–inch (20 x 30–cm) baking dish.

Pat the cod fillets dry with paper towels, then lay the fillets in the prepared baking dish. Pour the salsa over the top of the fish, then sprinkle evenly with Cheddar cheese. Bake, uncovered, in the oven for 15 minutes, or until the fish is flaky.

Top the cod with sliced avocado, crème fraîche and cilantro. Serve with pan-toasted asparagus (if using).

Chef's Notes: If you would like some extra crunch, you could top the baked cod with store-bought zucchini chips.

If using asparagus, heat 2 teaspoons (10 ml) of olive oil in a skillet over medium-high heat. Cut and discard the ends of the asparagus and season with salt. Toast in the skillet for 4 to 5 minutes until brown.

Palmini Shrimp Scampi

Believe it, my dear friends, you can definitely have pasta for dinner while keeping it low carb and full of flavor. Palmini is a low-carb pasta alternative made from hearts of palm. The additional flavor notes of dry pinot grigio, Italian seasoning, butter and a dash of cream all come together to make this dish quick, hearty and delicious.

Serves 4

2 (14-oz [397-g]) cans palmini linguine

2 tbsp (28 g) unsalted grass-fed butter

2 cloves garlic, minced

½ cup (120 ml) white wine, such as pinot grigio

4–5 cups (1–1.2 kg) raw shrimp, peeled and deveined

¼ tsp kosher salt

¼ tsp ground black pepper

¼ cup (60 ml) heavy cream

2 tsp (1 g) Italian seasoning

2–3 sprigs of fresh thyme (optional)

Strain the palmini and rinse thoroughly. In a medium-sized saucepan, boil the palmini in water for 10 minutes. If you don't like the veggie taste of the palmini, you can soak it in milk 1 hour prior to cooking or overnight, then rinse again before boiling. Discard the water and set the linguine aside.

Heat a 12-inch (30-cm) skillet over medium-high heat. Once heated, add the butter and garlic, then cook until fragrant, about 1 minute. Add the wine and cook until slightly reduced, about 1 minute. Toss the shrimp with salt and pepper and add it to the skillet.

Cook covered for about 2 minutes, until the shrimp is pink and cooked through. Add heavy cream and Italian seasoning, and cook for 1 minute. Turn the heat off and add the palmini to the skillet, coating it in the wine sauce.

Top with fresh thyme (if using), then transfer to a serving bowl and serve hot.

Meatless Mondays

Vegetarian meals, when done right, can be deliciously simple, economical and—of course—low carb. Some of my weeknight dinner favorites from this chapter are my Roasted Veggies and Sage-Garlic Pecans with Burrata (page 125) and my Eggplant Parmesan Bites (page 129), because you still get the benefits of a delicious, well-balanced meal, and you don't miss the meat. They are healthy, quick and delicious—just like all the recipes in this chapter. Plus, think of all the healthy gourmet delights we can create with cheese and eggs!

Roasted Veggies and Sage-Garlic Pecans with Burrata

Roasted veggies are great, but they wouldn't be complete without a generous helping of luxurious Burrata. Every component in this 30-minute low-carb spread is one to envy, from the citrus notes of sage to the nutty, buttery toasted pecans to the smoky char from the roasted vegetables. This is some serious eats.

Serves 4

2 cups (232 g) radishes, halved

2 cups (182 g) broccoli florets

1 zucchini, chopped

1 red bell pepper, sliced

3 cloves garlic, minced

4 large fresh sage leaves, finely chopped

½ tsp kosher salt

½ tsp ground black pepper

3 tbsp (45 ml) extra virgin olive oil

1 cup (109 g) pecan halves

1 tbsp (14 g) unsalted grass-fed butter, melted

2 (8-oz [226-g]) pieces of Burrata cheese

1 (15-oz [425-g]) can salted cannellini beans, drained and rinsed, for serving (optional)

Preheat the oven to 425°F (220°C, or gas mark 7). Line a baking sheet with parchment paper. Place the oven rack in the bottom position.

Add the radishes, broccoli, zucchini and bell pepper to a large bowl. Toss in the garlic, sage, salt, pepper and oil until coated. Lay out the veggies on the baking sheet and transfer to the preheated oven. Bake for 20 minutes.

Coat the pecans in the butter. When the veggies are close to the 15-minute mark, add the pecans to the baking sheet and bake for the final 5 minutes. Transfer to a serving plate and add the Burrata cheese. Serve with cannellini beans (if using).

Zucchini Ramen Noodle Soup

No matter what, you always found yourself eating ramen out of a microwaved bowl in college.
It was soupy noodles and not much else. Imagine if you found a veggie-based recipe
that was full of flavor, packed with protein, low carb and delicious.
That's exactly what this ramen is: healthy good food.

Serves 4

¼ cup (60 ml) sesame oil, divided

4 baby bok choy, quartered

2 tbsp (32 g) yellow miso paste (optional)

4 cloves garlic, minced

2 shallots, chopped

2 tbsp (12 g) minced fresh ginger

¼ cup (60 ml) coconut aminos

8 cups (1.9 L) vegetable broth

½ tsp kosher salt

4 zucchinis, spiralized

4–6 eggs, soft boiled, peeled and sliced

2 (3-oz [85-g]) packages enoki mushrooms

1 cup (50 g) scallions, diced (optional)

Heat 1 tablespoon (15 ml) of oil in a 12-inch (30-cm) skillet over medium-high heat. Add the bok choy to the skillet and cook for roughly 2 minutes on both sides until lightly charred. Remove the bok choy from the skillet and set it aside.

Add the remaining oil, then add the miso (if using), garlic, shallots, ginger and coconut aminos. Sauté for 3 minutes. Add the broth and salt, and bring to a simmer. Reduce the heat to low, then add the zucchini. Let the soup simmer for 5 minutes. Serve with the bok choy, eggs, enoki mushrooms and a topping of scallions, if using.

Chef's Note: For instructions on how to make soft-boiled eggs, refer to page 142.

Eggplant Parmesan Bites

Just when I thought eggplants couldn't get any more interesting, these delightful low-carb geniuses were born. These cheesy bites with a hint of basil will satisfy all your finger food and dinner cravings. Dip them in some marinara for some extra sauciness.

Serves 4

3 cups (312 g) almond flour, divided

3 eggs, beaten

1 cup (100 g) freshly grated Parmesan

1 tbsp (3 g) Italian seasoning

¼ tsp kosher salt

¼ tsp ground black pepper

2 medium eggplants, peeled and cubed

1 tbsp (3 g) chopped fresh basil, for serving

Marinara sauce, for serving

Low-carb creamy tomato soup, for serving (optional)

Preheat your oven to 375°F (190°C, or gas mark 5). Line a baking sheet with parchment paper.

Set up 3 bowls on the counter. In the first bowl, add 1 cup (104 g) of almond flour. In the second bowl, add the eggs. In the third bowl, add 2 cups (208 g) of almond flour, the Parmesan, Italian seasoning, salt and pepper.

Coat the eggplant cubes in almond flour, then dip them in eggs and then toss in the Parmesan mixture. Place the coated eggplant cubes on the baking sheet and transfer them to the oven. Bake for 25 minutes until golden brown.

Garnish with a sprinkle of basil and serve with marinara sauce for dipping. This pairs well with low-carb tomato soup for a heartier meal.

Asian Macadamia Nut Salad with Enoki

A fresh and low-carb weeknight salad with buttery hints of macadamia nuts, toasted sesame seeds and fresh enoki is nothing short of a palate pleaser. It's light and filling and requires minimal effort to put together. This is what weeknight cooking is all about.

Serves 2

Dressing

3 tbsp (45 ml) mayonnaise

1 tbsp (15 ml) rice vinegar

1 tbsp (15 ml) white wine vinegar

3 tbsp (45 ml) coconut aminos

1 tsp finely grated fresh ginger

1 tsp sesame oil

1 large clove garlic, minced

1 tsp Sriracha chili sauce

¼ tsp kosher salt

⅛ tsp ground black pepper

¼ cup (60 ml) hempseed oil

Salad

¾ cup (101 g) macadamia nuts

1½ tbsp (14 g) white sesame seeds

1 (¾-lb [340-g]) package field greens

1 (3-oz [85-g]) package enoki mushrooms, trimmed

To make the dressing: In a food processor, combine the mayonnaise, rice vinegar, white wine vinegar, coconut aminos, ginger, sesame oil, garlic, Sriracha, salt and pepper. While pulsing, gradually pour in the hempseed oil until the dressing is smooth. Set aside.

To make the salad, heat a skillet over medium-low heat. Toast the macadamia nuts until golden brown, 4 to 5 minutes. Remove the nuts from the skillet, and add the sesame seeds to the same skillet. Toast the sesame seeds until golden brown, 2 to 3 minutes. Transfer the sesame seeds to a plate and chop the macadamia nuts.

Assemble the salad with field greens, enoki mushrooms, macadamia nuts and sesame seeds. Top with the salad dressing.

Cauliflower Arrabbiata Casserole

Casseroles may not be a first-choice favorite when choosing a weeknight dinner, but my low-carb cauliflower arrabbiata may just make it to the top of your menu. This cheesy and saucy casserole is quick, delicious and slightly herby—and it will make you fall in love with casseroles all over again.

Serves 4

Olive oil spray or butter, for the dish

4 cups (400 g) fresh cauliflower florets

3 tbsp (40 g) coconut oil, melted and divided

Kosher salt and ground black pepper

½ cup (120 ml) store-bought organic arrabbiata sauce

1 cup (113 g) shredded sharp Cheddar cheese

¼ cup (60 ml) heavy cream

¼ cup (60 ml) unsweetened oat milk

2 tbsp (5 g) chopped fresh basil

Preheat your oven to 450°F (230°C, or gas mark 8). Lightly grease a 9-inch (23-cm) ovenproof casserole or Pyrex dish with oil spray or butter.

Toss the cauliflower florets in 2 tablespoons (30 ml) of the melted coconut oil and arrange the cauliflower in the casserole dish. Season with salt and pepper. Roast the cauliflower for 15 minutes until light brown and crisp. Pour the arrabbiata sauce over the cauliflower and keep warm.

In a small saucepan over medium heat, add the remaining coconut oil, cheese, heavy cream and oat milk. Season with a dash of salt and pepper. Heat until the cheese is melted and the mixture is smooth, 1 to 2 minutes. Remove from the heat immediately and pour over the cauliflower. Top with fresh basil and serve hot.

Chef's Note: Arrabbiata sauce is an Italian sauce made from garlic, tomatoes, dried red chili peppers and olive oil. It's commonly used as a pasta sauce similar to marinara.

Sharp Cheddar and Kale Frittata

For those moments when you're craving breakfast for dinner, this low-carb frittata is for you. It's a feel-good weeknight frittata packed with delicious cheesy protein and veggies—and, of course, it comes together in less than 30 minutes. Your leftovers will also make a great breakfast treat, if they last that long.

Serves 5

1 tbsp (15 ml) extra virgin olive oil

2 shallots, chopped

3 cups (201 g) chopped kale

1 cup (113 g) shredded aged Cheddar cheese

6 large eggs

¼ cup (60 ml) half-and-half

Kosher salt and ground black pepper

½ cup (30 g) chopped fresh parsley

Preheat your oven to 400°F (200°C, or gas mark 6).

Heat the oil in a 10-inch (25-cm) nonstick skillet over medium-high heat. Sauté the shallots and kale until the shallots are browned and the kale is withered, about 5 minutes. Top with the Cheddar cheese. Turn the heat off.

In a medium bowl, whisk together the eggs, half-and-half, salt and pepper. Pour the egg mixture into the skillet over the cheese and kale. Transfer to the oven and bake for 10 minutes. Remove the frittata from the oven and garnish with parsley.

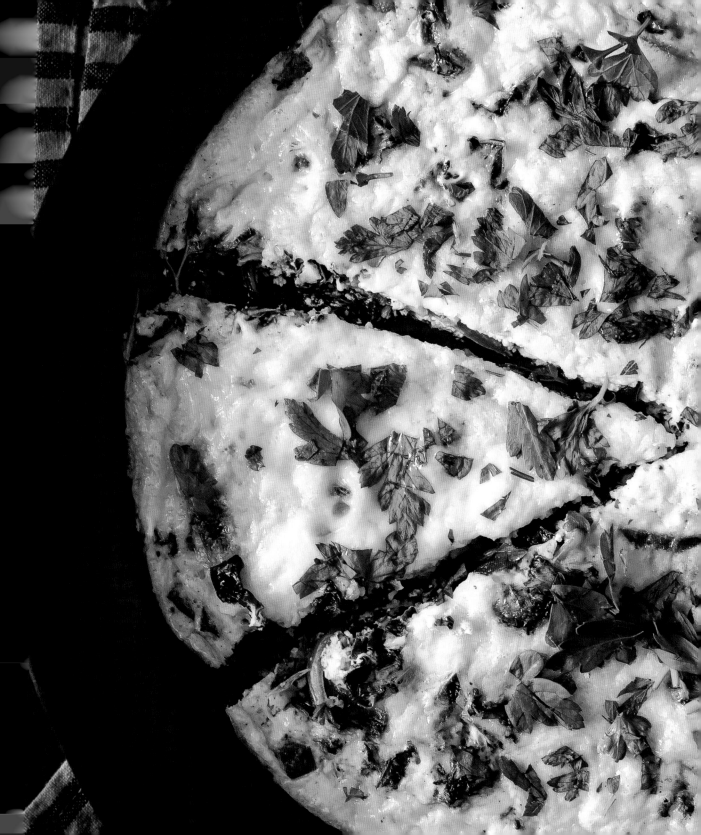

Pumpkin Cauliflower Mac and Cheese

Mac and cheese is a classic comfort food that never gets old, and you should be able to enjoy it every day with zero guilt and one hundred percent pleasure! And you can, thanks to the union of cauliflower, pumpkin seeds, Gouda and Cheddar cheese. It's low carb and simply made into a delicious bowl of happiness.

Serves 4

4 cups (400 g) fresh cauliflower florets

2 tbsp (30 ml) extra virgin olive oil

¼ tsp kosher salt, plus more for seasoning

¼ tsp ground black pepper, plus more for seasoning

½ cup (57 g) freshly grated Gouda cheese

½ cup (57 g) freshly grated Cheddar cheese

¼ cup (60 ml) heavy cream

¼ cup (60 ml) unsweetened cashew milk or other nut milk

1 tbsp (14 g) grass-fed butter, melted

2–3 tbsp (30–45 g) pumpkin puree

2 tbsp (18 g) pumpkin seeds (optional)

Preheat your oven to 450°F (230°C, or gas mark 8). Line a baking sheet with parchment paper. Place the oven rack on the bottom.

Toss the cauliflower florets in oil and place them on the parchment paper. Season with a dash of salt and pepper. Transfer the baking sheet to the oven and bake for 11 to 13 minutes. Transfer the cauliflower to a bowl and set it aside.

In a small saucepan over medium heat, add the Gouda, Cheddar, heavy cream, cashew milk, butter, ¼ teaspoon salt and ¼ teaspoon pepper. Heat until the cheese is melted and the mixture is smooth, about 1 to 2 minutes. Add the pumpkin puree and stir for about 30 seconds.

Remove the pan from the heat immediately and pour the sauce over the cauliflower. Toss until coated. Top with pumpkin seeds (if using) and serve hot.

Quiche Pepper Cups

Bell peppers are so juicy and sweet, and they are naturally low carb. They can also be stuffed with wonderful ingredients that are flavorful, delicious and quick to cook. Just try this quiche. In my opinion, it's a second cousin to a jalapeño popper.

Serves 4

2 tbsp (30 ml) extra virgin olive oil

4 eggs

½ cup (120 ml) heavy cream

½ cup (120 ml) unsweetened almond milk

½ tsp kosher salt

¼ tsp ground black pepper

1 tsp dried basil

2 large green bell peppers, halved

8 cherry tomatoes, halved

½ cup (57 g) freshly grated Cheddar cheese

Preheat your oven to 400°F (200°C, or gas mark 6). Grease a 9-inch (23-cm) casserole dish with the oil.

In a medium bowl, whisk the eggs. Add the heavy cream, almond milk, salt, pepper and basil. Whisk until combined.

Lay the peppers on the casserole dish, then fill them with cherry tomatoes and Cheddar cheese, distributed equally. Using a ⅓-cup (80-ml) measuring cup as a guide, divide the egg mixture between the pepper cups, making sure the egg mixture is equally distributed.

Transfer carefully to the oven so that the cups do not tilt. Bake for 25 minutes until golden. Serve hot.

Tofu-Cauliflower Curry Fried Rice

Of course, you cannot have a vegetarian low-carb meal without some tofu, especially when it's seasoned with curry and you get to enjoy all the flavors you love in curry fried rice. This low-carb dish comes together in under 30 minutes and is a weeknight favorite you and your family will love.

Serves 4

1 (14-oz [397-g]) block of firm tofu

4 tsp (20 ml) avocado oil, divided

1 red bell pepper, sliced

1 small red onion, sliced thin

2 cups (226 g) store-bought cauliflower rice

1 tbsp (6 g) curry powder, divided

½ tsp kosher salt

½ tsp ground black pepper

Cut the block of tofu in half. Place each half between 2 paper towels and gently squeeze each one to remove excess liquid.

Heat 2 teaspoons (10 ml) of oil in a 12-inch (30-cm) skillet over medium-high heat. Sauté the pepper, onion and cauliflower rice, 2 to 3 minutes. Add ½ tablespoon (3 g) of curry powder, then cook for 1 minute. Transfer the vegetables to a plate and wipe down the skillet, then set aside. You will be using the skillet to make the tofu.

Heat the remaining avocado oil in the same skillet over medium-high heat. Break apart the tofu into the pan using your hands until chunky, then scramble with a spoon until most of the water has dried out and the tofu turns golden brown, about 4 to 5 minutes.

Once the tofu is almost cooked (about 5 minutes), add the salt, pepper and the remaining curry powder. Add the cauliflower mixture to the skillet, stir gently to combine and let warm through for 2 minutes. Serve hot.

Asparagus and Eggs with Italian Dressing

This is an elegant low-carb dinner that has just the right amount of tanginess to leave your palate feeling refreshed. The asparagus is nice and crispy, and the eggs have a creamy yolk. Throw in some avocados and toasted almonds, and you've made a complete and hearty dinner.

Serves 4

Italian Dressing

¼ cup (60 ml) extra virgin olive oil

2 tbsp (30 ml) white wine vinegar

2 tbsp (8 g) chopped fresh Italian parsley

1 tbsp (15 ml) freshly squeezed lemon juice

2 cloves garlic, minced

1 tsp dried basil

¼ tsp red pepper flakes

⅛ tsp dried oregano

6–8 eggs

2 tbsp (30 ml) avocado oil

20 asparagus stalks, ends removed

2 avocados, peeled, pitted and sliced

⅔ cup (72 g) toasted almond slivers

To make the dressing: In a small bowl, add the oil, vinegar, parsley, lemon juice, garlic, basil, red pepper flakes and oregano. Whisk until combined, then set aside.

Prepare a medium bowl full of ice water and bring a medium-sized saucepan filled halfway with water to a boil. Gently lower the eggs into the boiling water one at a time, using a spoon. Cook for exactly 8 minutes on medium-high for a creamy yolk. Remove the eggs as soon as they are done and transfer them to the ice water. Set aside.

To peel the eggs, crackle the egg all over by lighting tapping it on your counter, then roll the egg gently between your hands to loosen the shell. Peel the egg starting at the large end. Dipping the eggs in the ice water will help remove the shell. Once peeled, slice the eggs vertically with a smooth knife.

Heat a skillet with the avocado oil over medium-high heat. Cook the asparagus for 4 to 5 minutes, turning it as it cooks, until light brown. You want your asparagus to have a nice snap.

Transfer the asparagus to a serving plate, and top it with the eggs, avocado slices and almonds. Finish with the Italian dressing and serve.

Crispy Black Pepper Tofu
with Avocado Salad

Tofu makes another lovely appearance. This time it's spicy and crispy with cracked black pepper and hints of garlic and ginger. The avocado salad cools down the palate and also adds a buttery flavor. You won't want to miss weeknight cooking or dining-in ever again. It's low carb, quick and oh so simple.

Serves 4

Black Pepper Tofu

1 (14-oz [397-g]) block firm tofu

2 tbsp (16 g) cornstarch

¼ cup (60 ml) coconut aminos

½ tsp kosher salt

½ tbsp (3 g) ground black pepper

½ tsp ground ginger

¼ cup (60 ml) avocado oil, divided

2 cloves garlic, minced

1 shallot, chopped

¼ cup (12 g) chopped scallions

Avocado Salad

1 avocado, peeled, pitted and sliced

1 (¾-lb [340-g]) package mixed greens

¾ cup (112 g) cherry tomatoes, halved

Dressing

¼ cup (60 ml) flaxseed oil

¼ cup (60 ml) balsamic vinegar

To make the tofu: Drain the brine from the tofu and press out any excess moisture using a paper towel. Slice the tofu into 1-inch (2.5-cm) cubes, place them in a large bowl and toss with the cornstarch.

In a medium bowl, whisk together the coconut aminos, salt, pepper and ginger. Set aside.

In a 12-inch (30-cm) skillet over medium-high heat, heat 2 tablespoons (30 ml) of avocado oil. Add the tofu and cook for 8 minutes until golden brown and crisp on all sides. Transfer the tofu to a plate and reduce the heat to medium. Add the remaining avocado oil to the hot skillet and sauté the garlic and shallot for 2 minutes until softened. Add back the tofu, then add in the coconut aminos mixture and coat the tofu in it. Cook for 2 to 3 minutes until fragrant. Turn the heat off and mix in the scallions.

To make the salad: Combine the avocado, mixed greens and tomatoes in a salad bowl. Set aside.

To make the dressing: Whisk to combine the flaxseed oil and balsamic vinegar in a small bowl.

Pour the dressing over the avocado salad, and serve with the black pepper tofu.

Zucchini with Basil-Walnut Pesto

This is one of those low-carb weeknight dinners that is so delicious and requires minimal effort. It's creamy with a hint of feta and only uses fresh herbs, oils, walnuts and veggies. It really doesn't get any better than this.

Serves 4

Basil-Walnut Pesto

1 cup (24 g) fresh basil leaves

⅓ cup (39 g) chopped raw walnuts

2 tbsp (18 g) raw pumpkin seeds (optional)

¼ cup (38 g) feta cheese

1 tsp chia seeds

¼ cup (60 ml) extra virgin olive oil, plus more if needed

Dash of chili powder

Tomato Zucchini

1 tbsp (15 ml) avocado oil

2 large zucchinis, spiralized

¾ cup (112 g) cherry tomatoes, halved

½ tsp kosher salt

¼ tsp ground black pepper

To make the pesto: Add the basil, walnuts, pumpkin seeds (if using), feta, chia seeds, oil and chili powder to a food processor. Puree until smooth. You may still see some tiny little walnut pieces, which is fine. If you feel your pesto is a little thick, add a little more oil until you get the desired consistency. Set aside.

To make the tomato zucchini: Heat the avocado oil in a 10-inch (25-cm) skillet over medium heat. Add the zucchinis, tomatoes, salt and pepper and cook until slightly withered, about 2 to 3 minutes. Add ¼ cup (60 ml) of walnut pesto and stir until combined. Transfer to a serving plate and enjoy.

Garlic-Thyme Butter Portobello Mushrooms

All the meatiness and a buttery, herby flavor but without the meat—and you won't miss it. These low-carb portobello mushrooms are pan-seared to perfection in less than 30 minutes, and they're topped with toasted almond slivers for an added protein boost.

Serves 4

⅔ cup (72 g) almond slivers

2 tbsp (30 ml) extra virgin olive oil

4 large portobello mushrooms, stems removed, and sliced

¼ tsp dried thyme

Dash of kosher salt and ground black pepper

1 large clove garlic, minced

2 tbsp (13 g) freshly grated Parmesan cheese, for serving

2 tbsp (8 g) chopped fresh parsley, for serving

2 (14-oz [397-g]) cans cooked palmini, for serving (optional)

Heat a 12-inch (30-cm) skillet over medium-high heat. Toast the almond slivers until light brown, then transfer to a dish and set aside.

In the same skillet, heat the oil over medium-high heat. Add the mushrooms, thyme, salt and pepper. Cook the mushrooms for 5 minutes undisturbed until slightly caramelized. Add the garlic and stir for 1 minute until fragrant.

Sprinkle with toasted almonds, Parmesan and parsley. Serve with cooked palmini (if using).

Chef's Note: For instructions on how to cook palmini, see page 120.

Cannellini-Tomato-Cucumber Salad

One of the things I love about cannellini beans is their rich and creamy texture. They are versatile, quite flavorful and suitable for a vegetarian diet. For those evenings when you feel like giving your stove a rest, this Buddha bowl of fresh greens with a side of creamy avocado dressing is all you need to end your weeknight happily.

Serves 4

Salad

4 cups (188 g) chopped romaine lettuce

4 cups (120 g) mixed greens

2 (15-oz [425-g]) cans cannellini beans, drained and rinsed

2 cups (300 g) cherry tomatoes, halved

1 large cucumber, sliced

1 (3-oz [85-g]) package enoki mushrooms

Avocado Dressing

1 large avocado, peeled and pitted

¼ cup (60 ml) flaxseed oil

½ cup (120 ml) white wine vinegar

1 tbsp (15 ml) water

1 clove garlic, minced

Dash of kosher salt and ground black pepper

To make the salad: In a large bowl, combine the lettuce, mixed greens, cannellini beans, tomatoes, cucumber and enoki mushrooms. Set aside.

To make the dressing: In a food processor, puree the avocado, flaxseed oil, vinegar, water, garlic, salt and pepper.

Pour a few tablespoons of avocado dressing over the salad.

Chef's Notes: Avocado dressing can be stored for 2 days in the refrigerator in a jar or airtight container.

You can substitute lemon juice for white wine vinegar and extra virgin olive oil for flaxseed oil.

Goat Cheese Zucchini Pizza Boats

The first time I made a zucchini pizza boat was years ago when I first started blogging, and I remember how excited I felt discovering the many healthy and creative ways zucchini could be made delicious. These delights are all the things you love about pizza, but without the carbs and all accomplished in less than 30 minutes.

Serves 4

4 zucchinis

Extra virgin olive oil, for brushing

Kosher salt and ground black pepper

1 (15-oz [425-g]) log goat cheese, crumbled

1 cup (240 ml) store-bought organic marinara sauce, or more to taste

¼ cup (25 g) freshly grated Parmesan cheese (optional)

½ cup (30 g) chopped fresh Italian parsley

Preheat your oven to 400°F (200°C, or gas mark 6). Line a baking sheet with parchment paper.

Slice your zucchinis lengthwise. Scoop out the seeds with a spoon until the zucchinis are hollow, then brush the edges with oil. Season with a pinch of salt and pepper, and place them on the baking sheet.

Spread goat cheese from top to bottom of each zucchini. You may not use all of the goat cheese depending on the size of the zucchinis. Spoon a few tablespoons of marinara sauce on top, then layer with the remaining goat cheese. Feel free to use more sauce if you find that the suggested serving size for the marinara isn't enough.

Place in the oven and bake for 10 minutes. Remove from the oven and top with Parmesan (if using) and fresh parsley.

Matar Paneer

Curry dishes are always a comforting favorite any time of the year, and so is this classic Indian vegetarian dish. With ingredients such as paneer cheese, enoki mushrooms, parsley and a spicy tomato sauce, this hearty weeknight meal packs a lot of delicious flavor and comes together in under 30 minutes.

Serves 4

1 tbsp (15 ml) grapeseed oil

8 oz (226 g) paneer, cut into 1-inch (2.5-cm) cubes

1 tbsp (6 g) grated fresh ginger

1 tsp ground cumin

1 tsp turmeric powder

1 tsp ground coriander

1 red chili pepper, finely sliced

½ (14-oz [397-g]) can diced tomatoes

Kosher salt and ground black pepper

4 cups (120 g) baby spinach

1 tsp garam masala

Chopped fresh cilantro, for serving

1 cup (64 g) enoki mushrooms, for serving (optional)

3 cups (340 g) cooked cauliflower rice, for serving

Heat the oil in a skillet over high heat until hot. Add the paneer and turn the heat down to medium-high. Fry the paneer on each side until it starts to brown at the edges. The paneer will brown rather quickly, so be attentive. Remove the paneer from the pan and pat dry with a paper towel. Set aside.

Put the ginger, cumin, turmeric, coriander and chili pepper in the pan, then cook for about 1 minute. Add the tomatoes, mashing them with a wooden spoon. Simmer for 5 minutes until the sauce is fragrant. Season with salt and pepper, if needed. Add the spinach and simmer for 1 to 2 minutes, then return the paneer to the skillet and sprinkle in the garam masala.

When ready, top with cilantro and enoki mushrooms (if using), and serve with a side of cauliflower rice.

Adaptogenic Beverages

Adaptogens are natural healing herbs that are used mainly for reducing stress. They are also good sources of antioxidants and act as anti-inflammatory agents. With low-carb diets, especially when you first start them, you may feel the physical effects as your body adapts to using healthy proteins and fat as fuel instead of carbs. Using adaptogenic herbs can help your body adapt to this stress, plus improve energy levels and cognitive function. Occasionally, adjusting to a low-carb diet can affect your sleep, and we all know that a good night's sleep is essential for overall good health, weight loss and muscle growth.

In this chapter, I will introduce you to some natural and accessible herbs, such as ashwagandha and reishi and show you how to turn them into delicious nighttime brews and tonics that you can make as quick after-dinner beverages. Whether you're ready to tuck in for the night or you just want to relax for a while, these low-carb beverages are quick and easy enough to do the magic.

Turmeric Golden Milk Tea

There's nothing more luxurious to look forward to after dinner than golden milk tea. This is low carb and sweet, and it's full of medicinal, antioxidant, stress-relieving properties that will give your immune system a good boost and get you ready for your next morning. It takes less than 30 minutes to make, so you might as well call it dessert.

Serves 8

4 tsp (9 g) turmeric powder

2 tsp (4 g) cardamom

⅛ tsp nutmeg

¼ tsp ground cloves

1½ tsp (3 g) ground ginger

2 cups (480 ml) water

2 cups (480 ml) unsweetened almond milk

¼–½ cup (48–96 g) natural monk fruit sugar

In a medium-sized saucepan, add the turmeric, cardamom, nutmeg, cloves, ginger and water. Boil over medium heat for 5 minutes, stirring frequently. Add the almond milk and cook for 5 minutes. When ready, add the monk fruit sugar to taste and stir.

Strain the tea with a strainer into a jug to get all the spice clumps from the bottom. Add more monk fruit, if desired. Serve hot, warm or cold.

Chef's Note: You can either use the monk fruit powder or sugar. The powder dissolves a lot quicker, but the sugar works just fine as well.

Monk fruit sugar is a natural sweetener derived from the fruit, which has zero net carbs, zero calories and is low glycemic. It also does not spike insulin levels which makes it diabetic friendly. Keep in mind that most monk fruit sugars are blended with erythritol, which is fine.

Chaga Hot Chocolate Milkshake

Who doesn't love a giant cup of delicious hot chocolate before bed? When it's low carb, good for you and only takes about 10 minutes to make, you'll be looking forward to bedtime just to slurp on this milkshake. Chaga mushroom powder helps restore your body's metabolic balance and reduces stress. When you combine it with ingredients like creamy coconut milk and almond butter, all you get is delicious.

Serves 4

2 tsp (4 g) chaga mushroom powder

3 cups (720 ml) boiling water

1 cup (240 ml) canned full-fat coconut milk or half-and-half

1 tbsp (6 g) raw cacao powder

¼ cup (65 g) organic almond butter

¼–½ cup (48–96 g) monk fruit sugar

Steep the chaga mushroom powder in boiling water in a small saucepan for 2 to 3 minutes. Pour it into a blender and add in the coconut milk, cacao powder, almond butter and monk fruit sugar to taste. Blend until creamy and enjoy. Add more monk fruit sugar, if desired.

Chef's Note: You can purchase chaga powder from online retailers. If you are pregnant, breastfeeding, diabetic, have a serious health condition or are on medications, consult with your doctor before purchasing chaga powder, even though it is relatively safe.

Ashwagandha Vanilla Tonic

Ashwagandha is basically the master manager of stress and insomnia. These conditions can occur when your body is adjusting to a low-carb diet, so this tonic is especially helpful. Ashwagandha is also quite accessible, so stock up on a pack and treat yourself to this delicious and velvety low-carb vanilla tonic. It is sweet, soothing and quick to make. Your body will thank you, and so will your bed.

Serves 4

1 cup (240 ml) water

1 cup plus 2 tbsp (270 ml) unsweetened oat milk

1½ tsp (5 g) ashwagandha powder

8–10 raw pistachios or macadamia nuts, soaked overnight

6–8 tsp (24–32 g) monk fruit sugar

½ tsp ground cinnamon, plus more to taste

½ tsp vanilla bean paste

In a blender, add the water, oat milk, ashwagandha, pistachios, monk fruit sugar, cinnamon and vanilla. Blend until smooth.

Pour the tonic into a medium-sized saucepan and heat over medium heat for 2 to 3 minutes, stirring occasionally. Top with more cinnamon, if desired.

Botanical Nighttime Soother

My good friend Kiki Athanas, a certified wellness educator on the use of adaptogens, collaborated with me on this fruity and delicious low-carb beverage. Together, we bring you a quick and simple nighttime soother with a dash of chamomile to act as a mild sleep inducer. The ashwagandha helps reduce stress and the dark cherries bring sweetness—all to guarantee you an evening of rest and calm.

Serves 4

1 cup (154 g) frozen, organic, pitted dark cherries

1 tsp ashwagandha powder

1 tsp monk fruit sugar (optional)

4 cups (960 ml) unsweetened oat milk

2 sticks Ceylon cinnamon

2 tsp (6 g) chamomile tea leaves or vanilla red rooibos leaves

Place the cherries in a microwave-safe dish and warm on high for 1 minute until warm and defrosted. Remove the cherries from the microwave and place them in the blender with the ashwagandha and monk fruit sugar (if using), but do not blend yet.

In a small saucepan over medium-high heat, heat the oat milk, cinnamon and chamomile for 5 to 8 minutes. Remove from the heat and discard the cinnamon stick. Using a strainer, pour the milk into the blender. Blend until smooth and frothy. Serve warm.

Sweet Tahini Elixir

A delicious, low-carb, velvety tea without the caffeine. This special elixir blends two amazing adaptogens, maca for mood and ashwagandha for relaxation, with a dash of cocoa, monk fruit and the creamy nuttiness of tahini. It's no wonder we all look forward to dessert.

Serves 4

4 cups (960 ml) unsweetened cashew milk

1 tbsp (15 g) maca powder

1 tbsp (5 g) cocoa powder

2 tsp (6 g) ashwagandha powder

4 tsp (20 g) tahini

2 tbsp (24 g) monk fruit sugar

Dash of cinnamon

Heat the milk in a medium-sized saucepan over medium heat. Whisk in the maca, cocoa, ashwagandha, tahini, monk fruit sugar and cinnamon. Continue stirring constantly until all the ingredients are immersed, about 5 to 7 minutes.

Transfer to a blender and blend until smooth. Serve warm.

Hazelnut-Gingerbread Bomb

Christmas comes but once a year. Although it's a celebration of yuletides and it's filled with joy, it can also be stressful. Take a break with my quick, low-carb hazelnut-gingerbread bomb. It's loaded with maca and reishi to enhance your mood and lower stress, so you never lose your Christmas spirit.

Serves 4

2 tbsp (30 ml) sulphite-free molasses

2 tbsp (32 g) hazelnut butter

3–4 tsp (12–16 g) monk fruit sugar

2 tbsp (30 ml) hot water

2 tsp (2 g) ground ginger

2 tsp (4 g) ground cinnamon, plus more for dusting

¼ tsp nutmeg

1 tsp maca powder

½ tsp reishi powder or chaga

4 cups (960 ml) unsweetened almond milk

1 cup (240 ml) unsweetened oat milk, frothed

In a small bowl, mix together the molasses, hazelnut butter, monk fruit sugar, water, ginger, cinnamon, nutmeg, maca and reishi until combined. Divide the mixture between 4 latte glasses or mugs. Set aside.

Heat the almond milk in a saucepan over medium heat. Once heated, turn the heat off and divide the almond milk between the glasses or mugs. Stir, then top with frothed oat milk. To froth the milk, warm it up in a saucepan, then use a manual frother, or blend on high speed for 1 minute. Dust with additional cinnamon.

Chef's Note: You can also use coffee for this recipe as a morning beverage. Simply substitute it for the unsweetened almond milk and follow the same measurements and instructions. You can add more monk fruit for extra sweetness.

With Gratitude

Success is nothing without the people who are always cheering you on, and a great many people helped me bring this book to life in all sorts of different ways. For that, you all have my deepest gratitude.

Foremost, to all the readers and followers of My Digital Kitchen.

My editor, Lauren Knowles, and the entire team at Page Street Publishing.

My cousin Chiaka Osuji, who is also my sister, recipe tester and occasional hard drive for all my food photos.

The Toronto Police Service and Toronto Paramedic Service; you guys saved my life. I thank you deeply.

The surgeons, doctors and nurses at St. Michael's Hospital, Toronto Rehab and Trillium Health. Without you guys, I wouldn't have been able to write this book.

My physiotherapists, Claire, Shriya, Talia, Catherine and Ed, who helped me get stronger.

My community coach Emily, who took me on all my grocery shopping adventures to test and photograph all the recipes for this book.

Kiki Athanas, a dear friend and holistic lifestyle and wellness enthusiast who collaborated with me on an amazing recipe for this book.

All the members of my family and to all of my friends, both near and far, for your graciousness and understanding when this project took up much of my time.

Teen Steeves, who is beside me in the photo. In the words of Tina Turner, "you're simply the best."

Francesca Young, for all your kindness and hospitality.

My mom, who is my number one fan, supporter and chief recipe tester. I love you.

My dear dad, you may not physically be on earth anymore, but your sweet soul gave me strength and courage to finish this project. This is for you, and I love you too.

About the Author

Valerie Azinge is the founder of My Digital Kitchen, a food blog and catering company with the mission to cater to multiple diets and happier, healthier lives. She has a robust social media following, and her recipes have been featured in BuzzFeed, the Food Network, the Huffington Post, Cooking Light digital magazine, feedfeed, MSN, Greatist and Vitamix Canada.

Index